ROMANOFF AND JULIET

ROMANOFF AND JULIET

by Peter Ustinov

WARNER CHAPPELL CLASSICS

WARNER CHAPPELL PLAYS

LONDON

A Warner Music Group Company

Romanoff and Juliet
First published in 1957
by Warner Chappell Plays Ltd (pka English Theatre Guild Ltd)
129 Park Street, London W1Y 3FA

This Warner Chappell Classics edition first published in 1995

ISBN 0 85676 054 4

Printed by Commercial Colour Press, London E7

Romanoff and Juliet was first presented by Linnit and Dunfee Ltd at the Picadilly Theatre on 17th May, 1956, with the following cast:

1st Soldier	Joe Gibbons
2nd Soldier	David Lodge
The General	Peter Ustinov
Hooper Moulsworth	John Phillips
Vadim Romanoff	Frederick Valk
Igor Romanoff	Michael David
Juliet	Katy Vail
The Spy	David Hurst
Beulah Moulsworth	Josephine Barrington
Evdokia Romanoff	Marianne Deeming
Marfa Zlotochienko	Dekphi Lawrence
Freddie Vanderstuyt	William Greene
The Archbishop	Edward Atienza

Directed by Denis Carey

Music for the ballads composed by Antony Hopkins

FOREWORD

In the original production, the two Embassies were
constructed on trucks which were fixed to the stage at one
point, so that the entire buildings could be pivoted on stage
and off easily and at will. This scheme proved eminently
satisfactory, as it enlarged the acting area considerably when
the interiors of the Embassies were not in use. It also enabled
the General to seem to push the Embassies out of his mind at
the end of the second act, when, at the climax of his
Herculean labour in the devious world of diplomacy, he
discovers that at last he has told the American Ambassador a
piece of news which the latter had not yet gleaned from
tapped wire or grapevine. This careless gesture of apparently
Samsonesque strength added to the meaning of the play by its
simple symbolism.

The crowd effects, fireworks and musical numbers in the third
act were, on the whole, left out in the London production, but
have been left in the script to give the reader an impression of
what was in the author's mind before the realities of a
theatrical budget cast their shadow over his hopes. In fact,
some of these diversions might only have confused the issue,
and the play is a perfectly practical proposition without them.

Peter Ustinov

November, 1956

ACT ONE

Dawn to morning.

The main square in the Capital City of the Smallest Country in Europe. It is dawn. Sombre building on the left with a balcony. Sombre building on the right with a balcony. In the background, a cathedral, with an illuminated clock, on which a great many unsteady saints frequently appear together with Father Time, Death the Reaper, and other allegorical figures, to hammer out fractions of the hour. The sky is expansive, and has the crystalline purity of early dawn in the south. Soldiers left and right, both in the shadows.

1ST SOLDIER	Your turn to start.
2ND SOLDIER	T.
1ST SOLDIER	R.
2ND SOLDIER	T. R . . . A.
1ST SOLDIER	N.
2ND SOLDIER	T. R. A. N . . . S.
1ST SOLDIER	U.
2ND SOLDIER	U? No such word.
1ST SOLDIER	Yes, there is.
2ND SOLDIER	Well, if there is, it's not spelled that way.
1ST SOLDIER	Yes, it is.
2ND SOLDIER	Ah!
1ST SOLDIER	Ah . . .
2ND SOLDIER	T. R. A. N. S. U. B.
1ST SOLDIER	S.
2ND SOLDIER	T.
1ST SOLDIER	A.

2ND SOLDIER   N.

1ST SOLDIER   T.

2ND SOLDIER   I.

1ST SOLDIER   A.

2ND SOLDIER   T.

1ST SOLDIER   I. Oh damn.

2ND SOLDIER   You should have foreseen that O. (*Long
                   pause.*) I said O.

1ST SOLDIER   I still don't think it's spelled that way.

2ND SOLDIER   Go on. Say it. N.

1ST SOLDIER   Transubstantiation? I'm sure it's got three
                   esses somewhere.

2ND SOLDIER   I gave you Rhododendron just now.
                   Although I'm damn sure there's only one H
                   in it.

1ST SOLDIER   Alright, alright. What's that make the score?

2ND SOLDIER   (*consulting a bit of paper awkwardly in the
                   dark*) Eight twenty four to seven sixty
                   seven.

1ST SOLDIER   Who's eight hundred and twenty four?

2ND SOLDIER   I am.

1ST SOLDIER   Bastard.

2ND SOLDIER   Well, I was eight twenty three before.
                   Stands to reason.

1ST SOLDIER   I won't argue. It only goes to show that the
                   night's too long.

2ND SOLDIER   It's nearly over. (*He consults his watch.*)
                   Death's late.

1ST SOLDIER	Death? They don't know how to oil him properly.
2ND SOLDIER	Your turn to start.
1ST SOLDIER	Oh hell. Z.
2ND SOLDIER	That's easy. E.
1ST SOLDIER	I suppose you're thinking of Zebra?
2ND SOLDIER	How did you guess?
1ST SOLDIER	Well — A.
2ND SOLDIER	What? A? Nonsense. Oh —
1ST SOLDIER	Ah.
2ND SOLDIER	(*murmuring*) Zeaa, Zeab, Zeac, Zead, Zeae, Zeaf, Zeag . . .
1ST SOLDIER	(*cruelly*) Take your time.
	(*A figure appears in the uniform of an operetta general, sky blue and silver. He wears a carnival mask around his neck.*)
2ND SOLDIER	Zeah, Zeai, Zeaf. Cave. A General.
GENERAL	Take your time. Finish your game.
2ND SOLDIER	I give up. L. What's that?
1ST SOLDIER	(*leering*) Eight twenty four to seven sixty eight. Now, where's my bloody rifle? It was here a moment ago.
2ND SOLDIER	My turn to give the order.
1ST SOLDIER	Ok, but hang on, let me find the — where the hell is it?
GENERAL	Getting warmer . . . warmer . . .
	(*The rifle drops with a clatter as the* SOLDIER *walks into it.*)

1ST SOLDIER	Got it. Fire ahead.
2ND SOLIDER	(*colloquial*) Regiment. Regiment, pre-sent — are you ready?
1ST SOLDIER	Yes, only hurry, it's heavy.
2ND SOLDIER	Pre-sent — ahms!
	(*They do so, with insulting untidiness, in their own time.*)
GENERAL	(*saluting*) Thank you very much. That was a kind thought.
1ST SOLDIER	Don't mention it.
GENERAL	(*takes out a heavy gold watch*) Any sign of Death yet?
2ND SOLDIER	No, sir.
GENERAL	I make him ten minutes late.
	(*There's a strange sound of creaking machinery.*)
	Listen!
	(*They all look at the clock. The wobbling figure of Death the Reaper emerges, and hits a bell with sickening force. The sound produced, however, is dull and unresonant.*)
1ST SOLDIER	He's getting old.
GENERAL	(*shrugging*) Fourteenth century. Hardly adolescent by our standards.
1ST SOLDIER	(*bitterly*) Our standards.
GENERAL	(*reasonably*) You must be a Socialist, young man.

1ST SOLDIER	Socialist Agrarian Reform Peasants' Industrial Party.
GENERAL	I've never heard of it.
1ST SOLDIER	I'm a founder member.
GENERAL	Do you vote?
1ST SOLDIER	Nearly every day.
GENERAL	That's what I like to hear. A true democrat.
1ST SOLDIER	We get time off to vote.
GENERAL	Yes, yes, of course. So do I.
2ND SOLDIER	I don't hold with his views, General.
GENERAL	Oh, perhaps you belong to my party?
2ND SOLDIER	The National Iron Fist. The Nif. (*He salutes strangely.*) We wear orange shirts . . . or we would do if we could afford them.
GENERAL	No, I'm afraid I don't know that either. I'm Rally of Unionist Separist Extremes, sometimes known as the R. U. S. E. Anyone — ?
1ST SOLDIER 2ND SOLDIER }	No, sorry.
GENERAL	How strange. It's the party at present in power.
1ST SOLDIER	There hasn't been a party in power since the ultimate dictatorship of last year's season.
GENERAL	I stand corrected. Of course, you are quite right. We govern by coalitions. What I meant to say is that we hold the casting vote in the present coalition. In fact, I am President of the Republic.

2ND SOLDIER   At the moment?

GENERAL   Yes. I have been for some ten hours.

1ST SOLDIER   You're doing well. (*Extends his right hand.*)

GENERAL   May I? (*Shakes* 1ST SOLDIER's *hand.*) Thank
                   you very much. (*With a sigh.*) Yes. We
                   judge a dog's life as being roughly one
                   seventh that of a man. But a president
                   doesn't even deserve a dog's life. His
                   expectancy is roughly one-seventh that of a
                   mayfly. (*He suddenly looks at the audience
                   and smiles.*) Look at us —

1ST SOLDIER   (*challenging the audience as they see it for
                   the first time*) Halt! Who goes there?

GENERAL   Put your rifles away.

2ND SOLDIER   It may be wiser. We're outnumbered.

1ST SOLDIER   Are those people out there in the shadows?

GENERAL   Yes, and we must be very polite to them —
                   we're entirely dependent on our tourist
                   trade. (*He addresses the audience.*) Good
                   evening — You will find us only on the
                   very best atlases, because we are the
                   smallest country left in Europe — and
                   when I say country, I don't mean
                   principality or grand duchy. I don't mean a
                   haven for gambling or income tax evasion
                   — I mean self-respecting country which
                   deserves, and sometimes, achieves a colour
                   of its own on the map — usually a
                   dyspeptic mint green, which misses the
                   outline of the frontier by a fraction of an
                   inch, so that one can almost hear the
                   printer saying "damn". Our population is
                   so small that it's not worth counting. We
                   have no cannons, we need no fodder. (*To*
                   2ND SOLDIER.) Don't fiddle with your rifle,
                   there's a sport. It's dangerous.

2ND SOLDIER   They're only blanks.

GENERAL	(*shocked*) I should hope so!
2ND SOLDIER	Well, I believe in armed force.
GENERAL	Oh, on statues, symbolised by a cluster of angels striding upwards into nowhere, there's nothing like it.
2ND SOLDIER	Do you mean that, as a General, you're not the tiniest bit ambitious for our military future?
GENERAL	I prefer our military past. The harm's done and there it is. As for being a General, well at the age of four with paper hats and wooden swords we're all Generals. Only some of us never grow out of it.
2ND SOLDIER	But — aren't you proud of the fact that we won the last war?
1ST SOLDIER	No one won the last war.
GENERAL	We tactfully declared war on Germany several hours before her surrender. As a consequence we were offered six acres of land which didn't belong to us by the grateful Allies. This we cleverly refused. And now we are on good terms with everyone.
1ST SOLDIER	You live in the past, General. Our future lies in the abolition of frontiers. The day will dawn when the workers will tear down the customs sheds, demolish the road blocks, and extend the hand of friendship across the artificial gulfs imposed by nationalist and capitalist warmongers.
GENERAL	(*sadly*) You read a great deal, don't you?
2ND SOLDIER	Our future lies in our discipline and in the cultivation of heroism in the very young. To my mind, every mother who has

successfully borne five children should be
given a free issue of toy bayonets by a
grateful nation.

GENERAL   And yet, my dear friends, our love for what
is ours is far subtler, far deeper than all
your silly foreign ideas. And I'll prove it to
you. I only have to start singing a folk song
for you two to join in, despite your better
judgement.

1ST SOLDIER ⎫   (*derisively*) Folk song!
2ND SOLDIER ⎭

GENERAL   (*singing softly, and with love*)

An angel weary of Paradise
Came down to visit Earth.
She floated over hill and dale
Til she heard laughter and mirth.

What is that ripple of happiness
That wafts through the trees like a song?
What is that shout of banners
Which crowns the distant throng?

It's our army of rocking horses
Off to a bloodless war.
It's our princes and captains
On their way to the sandy shore.

Our swords are made of good white wood,
Our castles are made of sand,
Our lances are made of plasticine,
We're off to defend our land!

The angel returned to Paradise
A younger, wiser girl,
And swore she'd never journey again
Her head was in a whirl.

For as the sky has its paradise
So the Earth has its pearl,
Our country! Our country!
The Earth has its pearl!

(*Gradually the other two have joined in, at first humming the melody, then singing elaborately and fluently in parts. They finish. A silence.*)

2ND SOLDIER   Well, we did it.

1ST SOLDIER   (*disgusted*) And to think the words are meaningless. They're nursery rhyme stuff, devoid of a social message.

GENERAL   (*serenely*) Social messages change according to social conditions, while nursery rhyme nonsense is eternal. It has set many a wise foot tapping, and has cradled the great men and the idiots of tomorrow in a lilting sleep.

(*A window of the building stage left opens with a clatter. An angry man in pyjamas and wearing rimless glasses looks out.*)

ANGRY MAN   Can't a guy get a decent night's rest round here? If it is not the cathedral clock, it's drunks.

GENERAL   Drunks? I beg your pardon, Ambassador.

ANGRY MAN   Who's that? Oh, Mr President — please forgive my outburst. It was a great party last night. Or should I say this morning.

GENERAL   Thank you.

ANGRY MAN   The idea of wearing masks was just great.

GENERAL   (*modest*) It's traditional.

ANGRY MAN   Hey! I still have mine on! What do you know? The damnedest thing! (*And indeed, a black mask adorns his forehead like the goggles of a motorcyclist.*) Well, sure makes me wish you had Independence Day every day.

GENERAL	We do, but we can't afford to celebrate it more than ten or fifteen times a year.
ANGRY MAN	Is that so?
GENERAL	We have gained our independence at least four hundred times, which makes us cumulatively the most independent people in Europe.
ANGRY MAN	Is that so? Well, that's certainly worth knowing.
GENERAL	Unfortunately, we have lost our independence even more frequently.
ANGRY MAN	Is that a fact? You sure live and learn.
WOMAN	(*voice, hooting*) Hooper!
ANGRY MAN	Coming, Sugar.
WOMAN	(*voice*) Are you crazy, standing in that window with your arthritis?
ANGRY MAN	(*sheepish*) Well, I guess you fellas heard. See you. (*He disappears.*)
1ST SOLDIER	(*sour*) Warmonger!
	(*The opposite window opens, and another angry man looks out.*)
2ND ANGRY MAN	Pssst!
GENERAL	Ambassador! Good morning.
2ND ANGRY MAN	He said something?
GENERAL	Who?
2ND ANGRY MAN	Him. He —
GENERAL	Not much, no.
2ND ANGRY MAN	I can hear him speak if I put my ear to the window, but I can only catch the sounds, not the words.

GENERAL	We woke him up with our singing. I hope we didn't do the same to you.
2ND ANGRY MAN	I don't sleep.
GENERAL	Never?
2ND ANGRY MAN	Never.
GENERAL	Insomnia?
2ND ANGRY MAN	Policy.
GENERAL	Gracious.
2ND ANGRY MAN	May I congratulate you, Mr President, on the reception last night, which perceptibly increased our solidarity?
GENERAL	I enjoyed it. I was the last to leave, and got rather drunk.
2ND ANGRY MAN	(*without humour*) Drunkenness in pursuit of solidarity is not a sin.
WOMAN	(*voice, strident*) Vadim!
2ND ANGRY MAN	Da, golubchick.
WOMAN	(*voice*) Paidi Suda!
2ND ANGRY MAN	(*conciliatory*) Sichas . . .
GENERAL	You'd better go.
2ND ANGRY MAN	(*suspicious*) You understand our language?
GENERAL	I understand . . . the situation.
	(*Abruptly the* 2ND ANGRY MAN *disappears. A decrepit saint strikes the bell.*)
	St Simon Stylites . . . I make it seven sixteen.
1ST SOLDIER	Seven four.

2ND SOLDIER   A quarter to eight.

                (*They put their watches away.*)

GENERAL   Oh, well, St Simon never had much use for
                time, up there on his giddy column.

1ST SOLDIER   That clock's a national disgrace.

2ND SOLDIER   For once I agree with you.

GENERAL   Why? The only one who's always punctual
                is Death . . . whatever the time he always
                strikes his knell at the first streak of dawn
                . . . and believe me, he knows what he's
                doing. How I hate the dawn! It's the hour
                of the firing squad. The last glass of
                brandy. The ultimate cigarette. The final
                wish. All the hideously calculated
                hypocrisy of men when they commit a
                murder in the name of justice. Then it's the
                time of Death on a grander scale, the hour
                of the great offensives . . . fix your
                bayonets, boys . . . Gentlemen, synchronise
                your watches . . . in ten seconds' time the
                barrage starts . . . a thousand men are
                destined to die in order to capture a
                farmhouse no one has lived in for years . . .
                And finally, dawn is the herald of the day,
                our twelve hours of unimportance, when we
                have to cede to the pressures of the powers,
                smile at people we have every reason but
                expediency to detest . . . A diplomat these
                days is nothing but a head waiter who's
                allowed to sit down occasionally . . .
                (*Playing to the house on the audience's
                left.*) Yes sir, and how do you want your
                imports, in oil? In petrol! Underdone?
                Overdone. If I may say so sir, your taste is
                impeccable. May I say so, sir? Thank you
                very much. (*Playing to the house on the
                audience's right.*) Yes sir, of course, I
                guarantee not to serve the other customer
                any secrets . . . I'll tell him secrets are off
                the menu — although you and I know,

don't we sir, that — ? Ha, ha, ha.
(*Surprised.*) Sir, service is included . . . Oh
well . . . if you insist . . . (*With elaborate
gratitude.*) Thank you very much . . . (*He
comes up from his deep reverence and
looks searchingly at the soldiers.*) You hate
the night because you find it boring . . . I
hate the day because it's an insult to my
intelligence, a slur on my honour, and a
worm in the heart of my integrity, whereas
the night . . . (*He basks in his thought.*)
The night is marvellous . . . because it is
the time when the great powers are asleep,
recovering their energies for the horrors of
the ensuing day . . . and in that time of
magic and of mystery, our horizons are
infinite . . . they stretch not only to the
north, south, east and west, but up towards
the moon, down towards the centre of the
earth. In peace, and in harmony with
nature, we send out our vast battalions to
colonize the imagination . . . When others
sleep, our Empire knows no bounds.

(*A cock crows. The street lamps go out.*)

(*heavily*) There. Our daily winter has begun.

2ND SOLDIER   (*softly*) Look.

GENERAL   Oh, look.

(*A pair of lovers wander into the square,
too involved in each other to know where
they are. They wear evening dress, and
masks dangle round their necks.*)

(*softly, heartfelt*) Oh, I hope they found
each other very early in the night, for now
he may notice a wrinkle under the weary
longing eye, while she may spy a trace of
cruel satisfaction around his mouth.
(*Sadly.*) Ah, the morning after! Ah, dawn!
Let us be tactful.

1ST SOLDIER	My turn to give the order.
GENERAL	Ssssh! Dismiss, but for goodness sake don't do it as you were taught.
1ST SOLDIER	(*whispering*) Regiment. Salute the flag! Dismiss!
	(*They march off on tiptoe with a last sentimental look at the lovers. The lovers break from a long, long kiss and look at each other in adoration.*)
HE	Are there words which have not been used before?
SHE	There are silences which have not been shared before. Why do you look at me so critically?
HE	Critically?
SHE	Are there bags under my eyes?
HE	I would be lying if I told you you weren't tired.
SHE	(*hiding her face*) Then don't look at me.
HE	(*lifting her face again*) I want to guess what you will look like at seventy.
SHE	It's late. We're getting silly. It's the sunlight and the weariness and the sad farewell of old champagne on the tongue. There was no edge to our thoughts when the candles and the cut-glass ornaments sent shivering milky-ways up to the ceiling, and when your eyes sparkled like mineral wealth from the rock of your face.
HE	(*sadly*) You can't recapture it by language.
SHE	I know.

HE	Enchantment fades so quickly that after five minutes you doubt if it was ever there.
SHE	Do you doubt it?
HE	No. I remember it.
SHE	(*desperate*) But I am still here!
HE	(*holding her*) Yes, a warm, a living thing, which I desire. Last night we were as one, creatures in a dream, selflessly united in an endless waltz. From now on we are opposed, a man and a woman in love — the greatest, most exhausting struggle in the world — two moths racing for the flame, two cannibals devouring each other.
SHE	Have you known many women?
HE	I am a sailor by profession.
SHE	Thank you for your honesty.
HE	(*smiles*) You're afraid that I will compare you to the others?
SHE	Inevitably.
HE	And what if I say that you are better?
SHE	That's not enough. I want to be alone.
HE	You have never kissed a man?
SHE	Only four. And Freddie.
HE	Do you mean only four, and Freddie? Or do you mean five?
SHE	(*surprised, she turns it over in her mind*) Five? No, I mean four, and Freddie.
HE	Who's Freddie?
SHE	(*enraptured*) You're jealous?

HE	This is daytime. Last night Freddie did not exist.
SHE	No, you're right, he didn't.
HE	I'm waiting for an answer.
SHE	Freddie? He's my fiancee.
HE	I see.
SHE	(*a little foolishly*) He's in refrigerators.
HE	I don't understand.
SHE	He makes refrigerators. His father made refrigerators before him.
HE	A hereditary gift.
SHE	Yes. His father invented a device which can — now let me get it straight — boil, broil, fry, or freeze, all more or less at the same time — it works off the television — well, Freddie's father invented that — or rather, he had it invented for him.
HE	An inventor by proxy.
SHE	Yes. Freddie believes he has a mission in refrigeration. He told me once when he was drunk that in the event of war, he has a device which can freeze the Gulf Stream, and make everyone but us very uncomfortable. Oh, my God, I shouldn't be telling you this, should I?
HE	No.
SHE	You have no accent, darling. I keep forgetting who you are.
HE	(*with pomp*) I serve aboard the icebreaker Red October. Ironic, isn't it, that it may one day be my duty to crash through Freddie's most cherished daydream.

SHE	Oh, how awful. Now everything's spoiled.
HE	(*kindly*) Why? Surely love recognises no didactic frontiers.
SHE	No, it doesn't, but what a ghastly way of saying so.
HE	Ghastly? What is so ghastly about a clear thought, clearly expressed?
SHE	(*desperate*) But Igor! Creatures in a dream, selflessly united in an endless waltz —
HE	I said that, didn't I?
SHE	Yes.
HE	Curious how romance tricks the otherwise logical mind into inaccuracies. Naturally, the waltz could not have been endless, otherwise it would still be going on — (*As he sees her incredulous face.*) — and that is impossible since we are now here.
SHE	(*in real agony*) Oh no!
HE	(*suddenly*) Does what I say sound very humourless and . . . un-Western when I talk like that? (*Silence.*) I must apologize. I can never regret a phenomenon as beautiful or as powerful as our love, but I must admit that it has created within me the most reprehensible ideological confusion. I must consult my textbooks before I can hope to interpret to you in scientific terms the exact extent of my spiritual deviation.
SHE	(*hopeful*) You mean you love me more than Marx?
HE	(*sharply*) Please do not speak sarcastically. It doesn't suit you.
SHE	I'm sorry but I'm jealous of the man.

HE   I do not make light of your beliefs.

SHE   (*tenderly*) I can't make you out.

HE   (*running his hands through his hair in agony*) I can't make myself out. It's all so simple in the Arctic.

SHE   Do you blame the climate, my darling?

HE   No. No, it's relatively simple in the Black Sea also.

SHE   You blame dry land then?

HE   Yes. It must be that. Although a great deal of good solid work has been accomplished on dry land. That is undeniable. In fact, a considerable amount of Das Kapital was conceived in the British Museum, which makes it all the more remarkable.

SHE   Women? In general. Do they confuse you, dearest?

HE   Women? I've seen women before. I served on a ship under a woman captain, although in fairness to her, you wouldn't have guessed that she was a woman. She did not disturb me in the least. (*Slowly, with considerable difficulty.*) The fact is, I love you.

SHE   (*ecstatic*) Oh . . .

HE   (*severe*) Please don't interrupt me. For my own good, for our future, I must analyze my reasons for loving you in spite of vast and irreconcilable spiritual and political divergencies. First of all, we were wearing masks. Your mask could have hidden the eager face of a freckled collective-farm girl. When we tore then off at midnight, it was already too late. I was in love.

SHE   Oh, Igor, that's not true. No collective-farm girl has an American accent.

HE	Yes, I was cheating. Forgive me. (*Fierce.*) I must be honest with myself. I think I know what drew me irresistibly towards you.
SHE	(*coquettish*) What is it?
HE	(*very serious*) You couldn't possibly be the captain of a ship. You're one of the only women I've ever met who couldn't possibly be the captain of a ship.
SHE	Dad bought me a dinghy last fall. It's moored near Cape Cod. I love the sea, angel, just the way you do.
HE	(*gentle*) Could you bring a six-thousand ton cargo ship into Murmansk harbour . . . without a pilot . . . backwards in a snowstorm?
SHE	I've never tried.
HE	No, you couldn't. And nor could I. Glory to our woman trawler-captains.
SHE	Glory to them indeed. Kiss me.
HE	Not yet. I must first reach certain ethical conclusions.
SHE	Igor, there's so little time! (*To break his mood.*) I know what I like about you.
HE	What?
SHE	Your profile.
HE	The facade.
SHE	I never read a book unless I like the title. Igor, I like the title. I want to read the book.
HE	I fail to understand.
SHE	I like that, too. You could never understand.

HE	What?
SHE	All the things I have to understand. You could never understand why it's absolutely essential for the Chicago Cubs to beat the St Louis Cardinals in the next National League game.
HE	No, I don't understand. Why? And who are these Cardinals?
SHE	You have to live in Chicago to understand.
HE	I do not intend to live in Chicago.
SHE	Nor do I, but Freddie . . .
HE	Freddie again?
SHE	Oh, I don't want Freddie again. Kiss me.
HE	I forbid —
SHE	You want to.
HE	No.
SHE	Please!
HE	Thank you.

(*They embrace, and lose themselves in the silent game of love, oblivious to all around them. The* TWO SOLDIERS *reappear, one from either side, now dressed as peasants in rags. Both carry various merchandise. They see each other with some annoyance.*)

1ST SOLDIER	Aren't you resting?
2ND SOLDIER	It's too hot to sleep.
1ST SOLDIER	It didn't take you long to change into your street clothes.
2ND SOLDIER	The same might be said of you. I believe you tried to cash in on the market before I was properly up and about. Not a very

socialistic impulse, if I may say so.
(*Suddenly, cooing to the lovers.*)
Keepsakes, bangles, prehistoric coins,
religious postcards beautifully picked out
in silk and sequins.

1ST SOLDIER   (*angry*) You jumped the gun! (*Glutinous.*)
Peanuts, traditional salted marzipan, raffia
table-runners, English collar studs, back
numbers of *True Detective* magazine.

2ND SOLDIER   There's nothing more suitable to announce
your engagement to your friends than a
nice religious postcard. It takes away all
frivolous aspects from the negotiation, and
has a spontaneous dignity which no amount
of subsequent teasing can ever dispel. On
the other hand, If the minor prophets
picked out in petit point seem too formal
for the younger approach, shall we say, I
have a large selection of cards which fall
into the profane to saucy category —
milady surprised in her bath, in art colours
that will not run — Cupid's indiscretions,
a lovely series in a new Japanese
polychrome process, smuggled into the
country only last Wednesday —

1ST SOLDIER   No table is complete without raffia table-
runners and, incidentally, I can supply the
table as well. The clash of raffia and
mahogany may seem abrupt, and even
startling, to the eye as yet unattuned to
artistic adventure —

HE   Yes, but —

1ST SOLDIER   — Yet I am assured that even Paris, that
mecca of the beau-monde, is following,
albeit timidly, the trail we so boldly blazed.
No? Now, my friends, let us not be blind
idealists — love's first impulse quickly
deepens into habit — a habit which is
termed a "mature understanding between

two people." It is at this second, and far more important, stage of marriage that these complete back numbers of *True Detective* will come in more than handy. Husband back home late, madam? Baby crying, sir? Here is a nerve-steadying remedy — tales of horror and revenge, at a quarter their original price!

SHE

(*desperate*) Oh, do please leave us alone!

2ND SOLDIER

This is a free country, madam. We have a right to share your privacy in a public place.

(*The lovers resume their interrupted kiss. The* GENERAL *enters in a morning suit.*)

GENERAL

What? Still at it? This must be what they call the real thing.

1ST SOLDIER

It must be. Death to commerce.

GENERAL

The real thing! And I don't even know the false thing! You live, and learn, that you know nothing.

SHE

(*spinning around, furious*) Oh, please!

GENERAL

(*amazed, adjusting his pince-nez*) Miss Moulsworth!

SHE

Sh! Don't tell Dad, please!

GENERAL

I envied your idyll without ever realizing it involved the much-admired Miss Juliet. Merciful heavens, Lieutenant Romanoff!

HE

Silence! (*He looks around nervously.*) I implore you not to say a word of this to anyone. If you do, my career is finished.

(*The* GENERAL *laughs.*)

Why do you laugh?

GENERAL	I began life as a ne'er-do-well, but was discovered cheating at cards, and so my career was finished. Look at me now.
HE	You are confusing me.
SHE	Oh, please, don't confuse him!
GENERAL	Are you really in love? I ask as an innocent, not as a technician.
SHE	Yes, only he won't let himself go. It's psychological. He's gotten to the stage of sorting out his emotions, and kind of freeing them from all those men, you know, Marx, Lenin, Trotsky.
HE	(*rising, violent*) Trotsky! I can never forgive you for that!
GENERAL	(*hastily*) She meant Engels. The names are somewhat similar. You need my help.
HE	No.
GENERAL	Yes, I can see from your utter misery, from your eagerness to misunderstand each other, and from your thoroughly bad temper, that this is the real thing. You wish to meet again tonight?
HE ⎫ SHE ⎭	No.
GENERAL	Yes, very well, I'll see what I can do. Tonight is the thousandth anniversary of our liberation from the Lithuanians.
1ST SOLDIER	Is it really? I thought —
GENERAL	Who cares for accuracy? It may not have been a thousand years ago, and it almost certainly wasn't the Lithuanians, but we celebrate whatever it was tonight, and that's an order.

2ND SOLDIER	With fireworks?
GENERAL	Naturally. With whatever we can afford. (*The* 2ND SOLDIER *produces a couple of rockets from his pocket to the disgust of the* 1ST SOLDIER.) Two fireworks. Well done. It will be dark at eight o'clock. Leave it to me.
HE ⎱ SHE ⎰	No!
GENERAL	Does eight o'clock seem very long to wait? I understand. Try not to be impatient.
HE	(*abruptly*) Goodbye.
GENERAL	That's right. This is no time for emotion. Bear your separation with fortitude.
SHE	I'm going.
GENERAL	That's it. Bite your lip, like a heroine.
	(*Without looking round, the lovers go to their respective Embassies. They are tempted to look back at the door.*)
	No, no, resist temptation! Orpheus, don't look back at Eurydice! There are only twelve hours of Hades. Earn your joy tonight!
	(*Precipitately, the lovers disappear. The* GENERAL *sighs romantically, the* SOLDIERS *dry their eyes.*)
	We're a sentimental people.
1ST SOLDIER	I'm glad I didn't sell any of those stinking table-runners . . . they deserve better . . .
2ND SOLDIER	And my postcards are in such bad taste . . .
GENERAL	Oh, my God! (*With sudden anguish.*) I thought of it as a love story, beautiful,

pure, simple. Simple? It's a diplomatic earthquake!

(*As he freezes, a* MAN *dressed as a spy enters, looking too anonymous to be possible. He goes quickly and silently to the* 2ND SOLDIER.)

SPY   Have they arrived?

2ND SOLDIER   Eh?

SPY   What I ordered.

2ND SOLDIER   Oh, it's you . . . yes . . . (*He produces a small packet or two, surreptitiously.*)

SPY   Is this all?

2ND SOLDIER   For the moment.

SPY   How much?

2ND SOLDIER   Eight hundred.

SPY   Too much.

2ND SOLDIER   They cost me almost that.

SPY   (*takes them*) Put them on my account.

2ND SOLDIER   But when — ?

SPY   You will be paid. And — you have seen nothing. I never talked to you. I don't exist.

(*The* SPY *vanishes into the Embassy, stage left.*)

1ST SOLDIER   What's all that? Since when have you had commercial relations with the Russians?

2ND SOLDIER   Even a fascist must live. I supply him with postcards.

1ST SOLDIER   Who is he?

2ND SOLDIER	Isn't it obvious?
GENERAL	(*suddenly*) Men, I need your help.
1ST SOLDIER	We're off duty.
GENERAL	We are all in the service of the God of love.
2ND SOLDIER	But we can't live on our military pay alone.
GENERAL	Well, claim at the Ministry. Do as I do. (*Suddenly.*) What kind of mercenary prattle is this? Just now you shed a tear for them. Is it in the traditions of our country to confuse love with high finance?
2ND SOLDIER	No it isn't. That's what's wrong with us.
GENERAL	What did you say? Lef . . . wait for it, left turn. In step this time. This is war. Left-right-left.

(*They go, as though on parade, on the double. As another saint comes out to hit the clock, the face of the American Embassy is flown to reveal* JULIET *sitting in an attitude of deep dejection in the small section of the drawing room which is seen. The door opens, and* AMBASSADOR MOULSWORTH *enters.*)

MOULSWORTH	Well, and how's my girl? Tired, heh? Don't I get my kiss? Hey, I got news to put the sparkle back in your eye.
JULIET	(*fiercely*) Dad, I've got to tell you.
MOULSWORTH	(*good-humoured*) Ok, and I won't tell Freddie.
JULIET	(*amazed*) You know then?
MOULSWORTH	Sure, I saw you . . . and let me tell you, you looked just great . . . standing there in the moonlight in that Paris-type exclusive dress . . . and let me tell you something,

the guy you were with . . . well, he was a tribute to your taste, and there's no reason on God's earth why Freddie should ever know . . .

JULIET   (*pale*) You liked Igor?

MOULSWORTH   Who's that?

JULIET   The boy I was with.

MOULSWORTH   Yeah. Swell physique. Great golfer, I bet. What was his name again?

JULIET   Igor.

MOULSWORTH   Well, what's in a name? I had a classmate called Epiphany. Anyway, that's all over now. (*He beams.*) Now, listen to this baby. Are you ready?

JULIET   (*emotional*) Pop, if you've got good news, give. Right now I need to hear it, but bad.

                (BEULAH MOULSWORTH *enters.*)

BEULAH   Have you told her, Hooper?

MOULSWORTH   (*tetchy*) I'm on the point of doing so, Beulah. Give a guy a break, (*Beaming.*) Great news, Julie —

BEULAH   And how's my daughter this morning? (*Smothers* JULIET *with kisses.*)

JULIET   Hi, mom.

BEULAH   What have you said to her?

MOULSWORTH   (pointed) Nothing yet. (*Beaming.*) Great news, Julie —

BEULAH   Great news indeed. You're a big girl now —

MOULSWORTH   (*with terrible patience*) Let me handle this, Beulah. Julie —

JULIET	Yes?
MOULSWORTH	Freddie.
JULIET	What about him?
MOULSWORTH	He's flying in on the midday clipper!
JULIET	(*pale*) Oh, no . . . (*She faints.*)
BEULAH	(*sarcastic*) You'll handle it, Beulah.
MOULSWORTH	What's the matter with her?
BEULAH	Get some water, Hooper. She's fainted.
MOULSWORTH	Fainted — that's impossible.
BEULAH	Get some water. There, there, mother's here, mother's here.
	(BEULAH *cradles* JULIET *in her arms.*)
	(*loud*) You're just the most tactful man I've ever met, that's all.
	(MOULSWORTH *returns with a glass of water.*)
MOULSWORTH	I am forthright. In Washington they call me Forthright Hoop Moulsworth. I've heard them.
BEULAH	Julie's a girl, Hooper. A girl. Girls don't go for forthrightness.
MOULSWORTH	How was I to know that!
BEULAH	(*with an embarrassing sweetness*) Girls thrive on a lingering uncertainty . . . on a tremulous half-doubt . . . I know. I was a girl myself.
MOULSWORTH	Beulah . . . if I ran my business the way you think . . . how is she?
BEULAH	Coming round, oh so slowly. She's sensitive.

MOULSWORTH   We're all sensitive. (*Beaming*.) How's my honey?

JULIET   (*softly*) Dad . . .

MOULSWORTH   Yeah, here I am, right here.

JULIET   I've got to tell you — I am not in love with Freddie.

MOULSWORTH   Not in — ? Now, wait a minute.

BEULAH   She must have calm, Hooper.

MOULSWORTH   So must I have calm.

BEULAH   Up to bed, my only sweet one.

JULIET   (*rising*) I'm going . . . but first I got to tell you . . . I'm in love with Igor.

BEULAH   (*a girl again*) There's someone else. What's he like?

JULIET   Dad saw him.

MOULSWORTH   Beulah, this is far too serious to accept as a matter of course. Remember, Freddie's flying out here at his own expense. Who is this other guy?

JULIET   Igor Vadimovitch Romanoff, the son of their ambassador.

MOULSWORTH   (*a great shout*) What?

JULIET   (*quiet*) I'll go lie down now — get some rest, if I can.

                (*She goes out. Long pause.*)

BEULAH   (*very quiet*) Maybe we didn't treat her right when she was a baby . . . maybe it's our fault —

MOULSWORTH   (*rising, pale*) I guess there comes a time in the life of every parent —

BEULAH

(*suddenly violent*) Oh, Hooper, this isn't a board meeting!

MOULSWORTH

(*shouting back*) She must know what she's doing to me . . . her father? Why, if this ever gets out! It's impossible. I don't believe it ever happened. And you can sit there and tell me —

BEULAH

The fault, dear Brutus —

MOULSWORTH

Don't quote at me! (*Pause.*) Beulah. We summon all our resources of tact and understanding.

BEULAH

I was never sold on Freddie being right for her.

MOULSWORTH

That is neither here nor there. Freddie's father rowed in my boat at Princeton, but I'm deliberately forgetting all that — all my personal loyalties. The fact is that our only daughter has fallen for a Commie — a Communist, Beulah — and when I say Communist, Beulah, I don't mean a guy who sent a food package to the wrong side in Spain — I mean the son of a high-ranking Soviet executive!

BEULAH

You always show everything up in its worst possible light.

MOULSWORTH

Good God, Beulah, don't be such a damned fool.

BEULAH

Oh, that wicked temper of yours! First degree mental cruelty!

(*Pause.* MOULSWORTH *walks about.*)

It may just be a girlish crush — a teenage urge.

MOULSWORTH

Julie's twenty.

BEULAH	Oh, Hooper, don't be so hideously unimaginative! She never had any of the usual teenage urges. She may be starting late.
MOULSWORTH	Yeah, that's it, a juvenile infatuation. Of course. Why didn't we think of that before?
BEULAH	And then again — it may be love.
MOULSWORTH	I don't want that word mentioned again. Come, my dear, let us, you and I, go talk to her, calmly and with a modicum of dignity. What we cannot achieve by our persuasiveness, let us achieve by our example. After all, we are her parents, and the scriptures declare in no uncertain terms that we command her honour and her obedience. One thing only I wish you to promise me before we go up to our daughter.
BEULAH	And what is that?
MOULSWORTH	That you keep your mouth shut and let me do the talking.
	(*They go.* JULIET, *who appeared in the upstairs room soon after she left her parents, is laid on her bed in an attitude of tragic resignation. The facade of the Embassy falls as the facade of the other Embassy rises.* IGOR *stands. The* SPY *sits at a table, a few pieces of paper stretched before him.*)
SPY	And?
IGOR	And . . . ? More I can't remember.
SPY	A confession of only eight pages? It appears as though you were still attempting to conceal something. (*Pause.*) Comrade Kotkov's recent confession ran to two

hundred and fourteen typewritten pages,
and was written in a clear, concise,
functional style. At the end, the reader had
a vivid impression of the author's inner
rottenness. It was a model of how such
documents should be prepared. (*Pause.*)
You have nothing to add? (*He sighs.*) Very
well, let me help you. There are some
comrades who can do nothing for
themselves. Page eight, line twenty three.
You claim that love guided your deviation.
(*He laughs.*) I had over-estimated your
intelligence, Lieutenant.

IGOR   Because I speak the truth, no doubt.

SPY   Love recognizes frontiers, just as do armies.

IGOR   Only cynicism has no bounds.

SPY   Explain yourself.

IGOR   If my thoughts are simplified even further
to suit your intellect, I shall soon be
reciting the alphabet.

SPY   (*deeply suspicious*) which alphabet — ours
or theirs?

IGOR   (*exasperated*) Oh, my God!

SPY   What name did you mention?

IGOR   When?

SPY   God, did I hear?

IGOR   Why not?

SPY   Are you a believer?

IGOR   I have a perfect right to believe if I wish.

SPY   I did not ask you whether you had a right
to believe. I asked whether you do believe.

IGOR   I don't see the difference.

SPY	All the difference in the world. In the old days it was criminal to believe. With the advent of democracy, we are now given the choice of belief or disbelief, but naturally we are put on our honour to make the right choice. Otherwise democracy would have no meaning.
IGOR	Oh, the devil take you.
	(The SPY *immediately crosses himself.)*
	What are you doing?
SPY	*(pleasantly, in spite of his nervousness)* Belief in the devil has never been forbidden by any regime.
	(The SOVIET AMBASSADOR *and* MRS ROMANOFF *enter.)*
ROMANOFF	Good morning.
EVDOKIA	Good morning.
ROMANOFF	What is there for breakfast?
EVDOKIA	Caviar.
ROMANOFF	Caviar, caviar, caviar. Is there no end to this monotony? *(Hastily.)* I say this with all deference to our splendid sturgeon fisheries and our modern canneries.
SPY	One moment. Another subject has priority. Your Excellency. I must denounce your son.
ROMANOFF	Again?
EVDOKIA	Just a minute. Women have equality. I demand to speak first.
SPY	The fact that women have equality gives them no special privileges, as they have in the West. You cannot expect to enjoy both

equality and the bourgeois myth of "ladies first."

EVDOKIA   I am the wife of an Ambassador. I have the right to speak first.

SPY   Only outside the Embassy. Within these walls the fact that I am your chauffeur is forgotten, and I revert to being a high ranking officer of the police.

ROMANOFF   Let him speak, Evdokia. It is more prudent. Let him denounce Igor before you denounce me.

EVDOKIA   How did you know I was going to denounce you?

ROMANOFF   No breakfast is complete without it.

SPY   Now —

IGOR   No! Let me denounce myself!

ROMANOFF   (*warmly*) That's the spirit. That's my son.

IGOR   I am in love!

EVDOKIA   (*scandalized*) A fine time you choose. I must say, with junior Captain Marfa Vassilievna Zlotochienko arriving today.

IGOR   With who arriving?

EVDOKIA   Your betrothed. The heroic commander of the sloop Dostoevsky.

IGOR   My betrothed? But I've never even heard of her.

ROMANOFF   We intended to introduce her to you before the marriage.

IGOR   I should hope so.

ROMANOFF   Don't be ridiculous, and start behaving like a spoiled child. I met your mother for the

first time at our wedding. There was no
time for surprise. We were both spared the
degradation of emotional behaviour.

IGOR

I refuse to marry this female!

EVDOKIA

You will do as you're told! We have noted
with considerable regret that you are prone
to unstable and introspective behaviour,
and that at times you are as self-pitying as
a fascist.

ROMANOFF

Evdokia, you are going too far!

EVDOKIA

Yes, and I know where he gets it from.
Talking in your sleep about imperial
occasions in St Petersburg. St Petersburg,
if you please, not even Petrograd.

SPY

Most interesting.

ROMANOFF

(*a pathetic figure*) I don't believe you.

EVDOKIA

You even sang a snatch of the Imperial
Anthem, and lay to attention in bed. Your
abrupt movement made the eiderdown slide
to the floor, and I had to get out of bed to
pick it up.

ROMANOFF

(*roused*) And what about you? Yesterday,
when I took you shopping, you lingered a
full quarter of an hour outside a shop
displaying French hats!

SPY

Oh, ho!

EVDOKIA

(*uncertain*) I did it to pour my scorn on them.

ROMANOFF

Yes, but while your mouth was muttering
malice, your eye was roving avariciously
over those odious shreds of tinsel. Deny it
if you can — you were dying to try them on!

EVDOKIA

(*after a terrible pause — a hunted woman*)
Have I not suffered enough in my life
without this? I was strong when I defied

the Cossacks and carried vital messages
under an arcade of knouts to the red sailors
of the Baltic Fleet. I was strong when I
distributed potato soup to our troops
through three days and three nights without
sleep. I have survived revolution, war,
pestilence and famine. Have I now
surrendered my dignity — to a hat?

SPY   (*slyly*) Well, have you?

EVDOKIA   (*emotionally*) Yes, I have. I have! I admit
               it. I — I confess! It is a tiny confection
               made up or three black feathers, with a
               coronet of cheeky silver lace. (*Defiant.*) I
               love that hat! Last week they removed it
               from the window, and I was nearly ill. I
               retired to my bed and wept. I thought they
               had sold it. Yesterday I passed the shop —
               and there it was again! My life suddenly
               had a new meaning for me. All
               unpleasantness was forgotten. I kissed my
               husband in the street.

ROMANOFF   Evdokia! That is how you gave yourself
               away. (*He kisses her on the forehead with
               emotion.*)

SPY   A most interesting revelation.

ROMANOFF   You underestimate us, my friend. Do you
               think that we are the only fallible beings
               here? What about this, which I discovered
               among your personal belongings? (*He
               produces an American magazine from his
               pocket.*)

SPY   (*trembling*) You have been through my
               suitcase?

ROMANOFF   You go through my desk every evening. I
               only returned the compliment. And what do
               I find? Decadent American magazines!
               Stories of drug addiction in Cincinnati!
               The adventures of lascivious spacemen!

And as if that were not sufficient —
postcards of an indisputably suggestive
nature, depicting the ruins of Pompeii in a
most unscholarly light, and dwelling with
shocking emphasis on the murky corridors
of the Follies. Explain yourself, comrade.

SPY   (*uncertain*) I collected this material in
               order to furnish the Party with proof of
               Western decadence.

ROMANOFF   The decadence of the West is well enough
               known by the Party not to need proof. Can
               you deny that these items constitute part of
               a vast and well-documented private
               collection?

SPY   I . . .

ROMANOFF   (*ferocious*) Confess!

SPY   (*with a cry*) Ah, that terrible word!
               (*Slowly, on his knees.*) I confess . . . but
               you cannot know the loneliness of a spy's
               life . . . everyone is frightened of me . . .
               women are only good and kind to me if
               they want me to overlook some
               indiscretion, and it's a calculated, a
               charmless, and a frightened love they give
               me . . . (*He weeps.*) To me, women
               surrender everything but their secrets, and
               their company makes me feel more lonely
               than I feel alone.

ROMANOFF   (*embarrassed*) Come, come, not before
               breakfast. Here's my handkerchief.

SPY   A handkerchief! When I could flood the
               Volga with my tears!

ROMANOFF   (*with some pride*) There is no doubt about
               it. No nation can confess as magnificently
               or as completely as we.

SPY   Ah, the relief, the relief!

ROMANOFF	Now, now, you are a most distinguished secret agent. We will forget your little lapse.
SPY	No, no! Never forget it! Ah, my soul. How good it is to suffer so remorselessly.
ROMANOFF	(*with some impatience*) What kind of architecture is this? One brick displaced, and the entire edifice collapses.
IGOR	You have more experience than we have, Father. You are older. I fall in love. The chauffeur gives in to his loneliness. Mother surrenders herself to a hat —
EVDOKIA	(*burying her head in her hands*) My hat! What a disgrace. (*A sudden horrified realisation.*) And it isn't even my hat!
IGOR	You, father, you only let yourself go at night when you dream of Leningrad.
ROMANOFF	Leningrad? St Petersburg. That is an historical fact, and not subversion. (*Dreamily.*) I remember the city in 1913. The light streaming through the windows of the Winter Palace into the snow.
IGOR	(*romantic*) You were outside, in the cold with the peasants.
ROMANOFF	I was inside, in the warmth, with the court — planning the revolution. I was the Party's inside man. My duties were to dance with the wives of army commanders, and surreptitiously find out the dispositions of their husband's units. It was delicious ...
IGOR	Then surely, father, with your experience, you can understand me when I tell you that I am in love — desperately, wholeheartedly, in love.

SPY	I understand you, brother.
EVDOKIA	Who is she? Some penniless local girl?
IGOR	Does it matter?
ROMANOFF	We — that is, your mother and I — wish you to marry well, my son, high up in the hierarchy.
IGOR	But that is snobbism!
EVDOKIA	Don't be ridiculous. Snobbism was abolished in 1917.
IGOR	I am in love with the daughter of an Ambassador!
EVDOKIA	(*ogling*) Just a moment. Which Ambassador?
IGOR	The Ambassador of the United States of America.
	(*A Terrible pause.*)
ROMANOFF	(*his voice breaking with emotion*) Are you aware of the words you have just uttered?
IGOR	(*standing stiffly to attention*) Yes, father. Otherwise I could not have uttered them.
ROMANOFF	(*suddenly losing all control, screaming*) Swine! (*Pause.*) Saboteur! (*Pause.*) Interventionist! (*Pause.*) Anarchist! (*Pause.*) Trotskyist! (*Pause — with a sob.*) My son!
	(*During each of these accusations, it seems as though tears are being scattered around the room like grain. The* AMBASSADOR, *scarlet with passion, shouts each word like a military order.*)
SPY	(*in ecstasy*) This surpasses all other confessions!

ROMANOFF	(*contorted with fury and yet with traces of compassion and contrition, almost hopefully*) Can you change your mind?
IGOR	(*stiff*) No, father.
ROMANOFF	(*with ill-concealed pride in his son*) You will go up to your room.
IGOR	Yes, father.
ROMANOFF	Why do you smile?
IGOR	I will not be alone. (*He goes, stiffly.*)
ROMANOFF	You!
SPY	Me?
ROMANOFF	Breakfast is laid for three. You will join us.
EVDOKIA	A spy at the dining table?
ROMANOFF	Evdokia, we have lost our son.
EVDOKIA	(*with a shriek*) Vadim!
ROMANOFF	(*calm as ice*) Caviar, you said? Let us enjoy it . . .
	(*As* IGOR *appears upstairs, the facade falls. Two people enter the square, one a huge and cheerful* AMERICAN, *the other a pretty but grim* RUSSIAN GIRL. *They are followed by the* TWO SOLDIERS.)
RUSSIAN GIRL	Thank you for allowing me to share your taxi.
AMERICAN	That's Ok. Anything else I can do for you?
RUSSIAN GIRL	(*coy*) No.
1ST SOLDIER	Peanuts, traditional salted marzipan, raffia table-runners, English collar-studs, back numbers of *True Detective* Magazine?
2ND SOLDIER	Keepsakes, bangles, prehistoric coins, religious postcards, beautifully picked out in silk and sequins?

RUSSIAN GIRL	You have no sociological novels?
1ST SOLDIER	No.
AMERICAN	And no flowers?
2ND SOLDIER	No.
AMERICAN	(*cheerfully*) Well, that's it. No flowers. (*Takes out a note.*) Give me something for that. Oh, anything. Bangles. Sure, that's fine. Just great. Do I get any change? Ok, I know the answer to that one. Americans. No change.
RUSSIAN GIRL	(*studying him keenly*) You are not thrifty.
AMERICAN	I'm in love.
RUSSIAN GIRL	All the more reason for thrift.
AMERICAN	See you, beautiful.
RUSSIAN GIRL	Goodbye, sir.
	(*They go to their respective Embassies, and enter. The* GENERAL *tiptoes quickly on to the stage.*)
GENERAL	Who were they?
1ST SOLDIER	Search me.
2ND SOLDIER	The plot thickens.
	(*Vaguely, like a chant, the words "Romanoff" and "Juliet" can be heard, very softly.*)
JULIET	Romanoff.
IGOR	Juliet.
GENERAL	Sh! What's that?
1ST SOLDIER	I can't hear —
GENERAL	Listen.

JULIET	Romanoff.
IGOR	Juliet.
2ND SOLDIER	It sounds like . . . Romanoff . . .
1ST SOLDIER	And . . . Juliet?
GENERAL	(*very softly*) Where's it coming from?
1ST SOLDIER	(*near one Embassy*) Up here.
GENERAL	Balconies? Then there's hope . . .

(*The figure of Death the Reaper wobbles out and strikes the bell.*)

1ST SOLDIER	It's Death!
GENERAL	Death again? Death at a quarter to nine?
1ST SOLDIER	. . . Eight thirty three?
2ND SOLDIER	. . . Nine fourteen?
GENERAL	It's the first time I've ever known Death make a mistake . . .

Curtain.

ACT TWO

Noon to afternoon.

It is later in the day. The light is no longer the pale silver of early morning, but has the deep orange glow which makes the sky intensely blue and the walls the colour of peaches. As the curtain rises the clock strikes three. The Embassy walls rise slowly. Both lower rooms are empty, but the upper rooms are occupied by JULIET *and* IGOR. *They are both in positions of romantic dejection. The* TWO SOLDIERS *lie lazily in the street. It is siesta time. One is asleep, the other strums lazily on a guitar. Their merchandise lies by their side.*

JULIET *is the first to come slowly to life.*

JULIET   Oh, why must the mind hover, a blind bee, over dead flowers? And yet, maybe I like my flowers dead . . . maybe I'm not the happy, open-minded daughter parents dream about . . . maybe I'm not the normal, healthy modern girl who makes a sane selection of a mate after mature consideration in a night club . . . Do I betray my age group by thinking? Am I old fashioned and just meant for tragedy? (*With profound self-pity, and a sudden interest.*) Oh, perhaps tragedy. (*She looks at a photo of Freddie.*) To look at a man . . . to visualise children with his eyes and my nose . . . Oh, Freddie, if only I hated you . . . but no, I like you . . . quite . . . in your silly, keen, determined way . . . I never quite know what you're being determined about, but that look makes older men call you promising. Freddie, you're a skyscraper of a guy. You'll hold our babies in all the right positions . . . You'll teach them baseball before they can walk and you'll teach them to count before they can read . . . only Freddie . . . I won't be those babies' mother . . . why? Because I like you, dear . . . and because I don't love you

. . . (*She drops the photo, and takes up an empty frame.*) Igor, I love you . . . but I don't really like you much . . . maybe the two don't go together . . . when I was small, I always swore I'd marry a man with blue eyes . . . your eyes are brown . . . brown like damp patches on the wall, like school book covers . . . and yet, when I look into them, I lose my way . . . I forget my discretion, my education, my table manners . . . (*She holds the empty frame close to her face and shuts her eyes.*) Oh Igor, the way the warmth creeps into those eyes against your better judgement . . . like a slow wave of sunshine washing up a pasture late on a winter afternoon . . . made more welcome by surprise . . .

(*She is lost in her reverie, and cries quietly.* IGOR *stirs and leaps to his feet with the violence of a romantic.*)

IGOR   Theory is a corset. I can no longer breathe. Was Karl Marx ever in love? Are there frontiers which even the greatest of teachers have never crossed? Would the barricades have attracted so many martyrs if love had been as easy to find as death? I wonder . . . For the first time in my life, I feel a coward. I love the sea, but I love a woman more. A woman? If I could take her home — if it were possible — they would criticise her frivolous and untheoretical mind. How I hate it myself at times. They would even criticise her looks — that vapidly romantic expression — those great grey eyes which ask endless questions, and which make me smile as I think of them — that concern with dress, with personal appearance — so unfeminine . . . and yet . . . as one who has been nurtured on the truth, the accurate, didactic truth, I must shout for the good of my Slavonic soul, "I am in love!" If I have to die for it, if I have to kiss the soil with frozen lips, I shall have known this exultation . . . and Juliet, the silences! Stretching so intimately into infinity, silences which seem to wander among the stars and among stray thoughts, reducing all mysteries to the shape of a sweet and knowing smile, exalting each tremulous flicker of an eyelash to a vast, unfathomable mystery. Juliet . . . the tender gravity of our silences! (*He turns his head away violently.*) Oh how undignified to feel the hot tears rolling down where rain and sleet hammer so ineffectually! Remember, in your lucid moments, Igor Vadimovitch Romanoff, that you are second-in-command of a warship . . .

(*He stands stiffly to attention — his back to the audience — then breaks his stance.*)

(*a broken man*) No, Igor Vadimovitch Romanoff . . . there are no lucid moments left . . . you are a man in love . . . (*He sits heavily.*)

JULIET   (*with sudden anger*) Oh, drink your vodka with your buddies. What do you care if I'm on the verge of suicide? You probably chalk up the number of your conquests on the hull of your ice-breaker. I can see you now, joking with your awful papa about how you insinuated your way into a reactionary's heart. I hate you! (*She picks up Freddie's photograph.*) Poor Freddie . . . I said such heartless things about you . . . (*She studies the photograph with compassion and tenderness.*) Oh Freddie, you're dreadful . . . (*She drops the photograph again.*) Forgive me . . . Igor, Freddie . . . both of you . . . I'm not . . . myself . . . (*She relapses again.*)

IGOR   (*he rises angrily*) And yet I doubt whether you have the capacity to suffer as I can

suffer . . . you come from a new and
superficial race . . . we have suffered from
time immemorial, and when necessary, we
fall into the bitter practice gracefully and
unnoticeably . . . no doubt you are seeking
consolation with your father, who is
successfully cheering you up by recounting
his exploits on the Stock Exchange . . . it is
your education I must blame, not you . . . I
know my duty . . . I will suffer for us both
. . . (*He sits and suffers.*)

JULIET   (*a murmur*) Oh Igor . . . Igor . . . Igor.

IGOR   (*a murmur*) Juliet . . . Juliet . . . Juliet.

(*They are lost in darkness as* HOOPER, BEULAH
and FREDDIE *enter the downstairs room.*)

FREDDIE   Well, when's the next plane back?

MOULSWORTH   You seem to take the whole ghastly
situation very lightly, if you don't mind my
saying so.

FREDDIE   I take it easy, sir. I've never forced anyone
to do anything they didn't want to do. Hell,
a girl can change her mind about a guy.
I've changed my mind about a good number
of girls.

BEULAH   Oh, it's all too dreadful . . . and to think
that Freddie has flown . . . how many miles
is it, Freddie?

FREDDIE   Four thousand.

BEULAH   Four thousand miles!

MOULSWORTH   That figure is beginning to annoy me,
Beulah. We've had it several times already.
You've even consulted an atlas.

FREDDIE   I made it four thousand miles two hundred
and seventeen miles, counting the trips to
the airport. But what the hell. I like flying.

MOULSWORTH	Exactly. He likes flying, Beulah. Now I knew your father, son.
FREDDIE	I know you did, sir . . . and he knew you.
MOULSWORTH	He did indeed . . . and what's more . . . I liked him.
FREDDIE	I never talked about it with him, sir . . . But I'm pretty certain he liked you.
MOULSWORTH	(*a little irritated*) I talked to him about it. He did like me. He liked me a lot. He was a fine, upstanding man, and the best Number Three ever to row for Princeton. Now, young man, let me tell you right here from the shoulder what your father would have done under those circumstances. He'd have gone up those stairs and he'd have shouted his way into the girl's heart.
FREDDIE	I beg to differ with you, sir. Dad was a gentleman. He'd never have raised his voice against a lady.
BEULAH	(*in triumph*) There!
MOULSWORTH	(*to his wife*) What are you so happy about? Just stabbing me in the back all the way down the line.
FREDDIE	Dad would have gone right out there and clobbered that Russian.
BEULAH	Ho, how romantic!
FREDDIE	Yes ma'am. He was of the "let-the-best-man-win" school. He always won. He weighed 'most three hundred pounds.
BEULAH	Maybe that's the solution. Women just adore brave men. Look at the bullfighters.
MOULSWORTH	What the hell have bullfighters got to do with it? D'you think I want an international incident on my hands?

FREDDIE	No, and then I'm not a scrapper. I studied law for half a year. I'm a firm believer in negotiation.
MOULSWORTH	Good God, man. The days of negotiation for a wife are over. Nowadays marriage, like everything else, is strictly business, and business is pressure. Go up there, son, and fight for your wife. Start shouting, or you'll lose her to the next customer.
FREDDIE	Mrs Moulsworth . . .
BEULAH	Yes, dear?
FREDDIE	I'll do anything you think wise within reason. I'm deeply attached to your daughter, but I think it only fair to tell you that when I asked her to marry me she never said more in reply than that she'd think it over.
MOULSWORTH	In business that's tantamount to an acceptance. She may argue the terms of the contract, but she's initialled the rough draft, that's how I see it. Son, go up there and clinch that deal.
BEULAH	Oh, Hooper, do stop seeing everything in terms of business. When he proposed to me, he slapped me on the back, and said, "Beulah, how about going into partnership?" Then when Juliet came, I woke up to find him standing at the foot of the bed with some flowers. The first words I heard him utter as I came out of the haze and the agony were, "Well, first one off the production line."
MOULSWORTH	Well, I got you, didn't I? That just proves my point.
BEULAH	(her eyes shut in exquisite suffering) There is such a thing in life as beauty, Hooper.

It's a very wonderful thing. And your life has been the poorer for the lack of it.

MOULSWORTH (*loud*) I like beauty when it's practical, Beulah. I like a beautiful swimming pool, but only if it's got water in it. I like a beautiful marriage, but I'll still breath a whale of a sigh of relief when both parties have said "I do." Now, son, are you going to let me down?

FREDDIE (*good-naturedly*) I hate to say this to you, sir, but it's my marriage, not yours.

MOULSWORTH No, sir. The blue chips are down. I'm talking to you and appealing to you as one good American to another. Julie's a girl we both love and cherish, I as a father, you as a man who found it in himself to propose marriage to her. Son, she's drifting out of our life. She's in love with a Communist. If this thing goes through, it may mean that she could be guilty of attempting to destroy the government of the United States by force.

FREDDIE Oh, that's ridiculous.

MOULSWORTH It may sound ridiculous to you and to me, but it won't sound so ridiculous before a Federal Investigating Committee. And that's what we'd have to face, all of us . . . indictments, suspicions . . . ruin . . . and all because of her stubbornness . . .

FREDDIE Well, what d'you want me to do, sir? Talk to her? Or marry her?

MOULSWORTH (*after a short pause*) Whatever you think best, son. You're right. I was kind of hasty and . . . well, I'm a little sore about what has happened . . . It all seemed so great before breakfast . . .

FREDDIE (*with a deep grave sigh*) I guess that's . . . life.

MOULSWORTH   (*with a reciprocal laugh*) Never said a truer
                  word, son. That's what it is. Life. The
                  Mighty Unpredictable.

FREDDIE   Just at the start of the home run, why, you
                  have to break your ankle.

MOULSWORTH   Precisely right.

FREDDIE   (*rising*) Well, I'll go up there. Talk to her.

MOULSWORTH   (*extending his hand, moved*) That's my boy.
                  Put it there.

BEULAH   (*who has been lost in profound reverie*)
                  One small question, Freddie. If she changes
                  her mind and wants to have you, what will
                  you do?

FREDDIE   Oh, I'll marry her. I believe in marriage,
                  Mrs Moulsworth.

BEULAH   And do you believe in love?

FREDDIE   (*as though it were unimportant*) Sure, Sure.

BEULAH   Then go up there, and our blessings go with
                  you. Freddie, be gentle.

MOULSWORTH   Yeah, be gentle, but don't forget to be real
                  tough.

                  (FREDDIE *goes*.)

                  Goddamn gutless generation. If it wasn't
                  for the fact that I'm a diplomat, I'd have
                  shot my mouth off. His girl going to marry
                  a Red, and he talks about negotiation where
                  possible, all six-foot-six of him sits there
                  looking solemn and pious, talking of
                  negotiation where possible.

BEULAH   He's very sensitive.

MOULSWORTH	You always say that. A little mousy guy I can understand being sensitive, but a guy his size just hasn't the right.
BEULAH	Ssssh!

(*They both look at the ceiling.* FREDDIE *has knocked at* JULIET'S *door.* JULIET *stirs.*)

FREDDIE	Julie . . . it's me . . . Freddie.
JULIET	Go away, Freddie . . . I'm not in a state to see anybody.
FREDDIE	I only wanted to say goodbye, kid . . . I've come four thousand miles to say it.
JULIET	D'you mean that?
FREDDIE	Sure. I understand.
JULIET	Are you alone?
FREDDIE	I swear it.
JULIET	I'll let you in for a moment, Freddie, if you promise not to look at me.
FREDDIE	That's a tough assignment but . . . I promise.

(*She unlocks the door.* FREDDIE *enters.*)

Julie!

JULIET	(*her back to him*) You promised!
FREDDIE	Sure. Well I — well, there's really not much to say.
JULIET	How's business?
FREDDIE	How the hell do I know. Dad bought up most all of his competitors before he died. There's nothing left for me to do.
JULIET	You mean you've gone sour on refrigerators?

FREDDIE   I guess I'm just . . . mature. (*Sees his photograph.*) Hey, where'd you get that awful photograph?

JULIET   I don't know . . . I had it.

FREDDIE   No wonder you fell out of love.

JULIET   (*pained and weary*) Is Dad very upset?

FREDDIE   Yes . . . I guess he is . . . (*Without much enthusiasm.*) He's a great guy.

JULIET   (*dull*) The greatest. What can I do?

FREDDIE   (*he smiles*) I know what I'd do, but then I'm not you, and I don't think any advice of mine would be much value to you.

JULIET   (*to him for the first time, with a kind of interest*) Freddie, you've changed.

FREDDIE   (*with charm*) Have I? (*Not looking at her.*) Hey, Julie, what's it like being in love? Really in love?

JULIET   Hell.

FREDDIE   Is that so? I Gee, I'm sorry.

JULIET   What are you going to do now?

FREDDIE   Oh, I don't know. Marry. Settle down.

JULIET   Anyone in mind?

FREDDIE   (*smiling*) Never less than six. Put it down to my business training.

JULIET   I envy all six.

FREDDIE   That's sweet of you.

           (*Pause.*)

BEULAH   They're talking. I can hear the voices.

MOULSWORTH	That's not talk, that's mumbling. He'll never get to first base that way.
FREDDIE	Do you want me to go?
JULIET	Not particularly.
FREDDIE	I think maybe I ought to anyway.
JULIET	Aren't you going to tell me I'm crazy and unpatriotic to fall for a Commie?
FREDDIE	No. I'm not going to tell you that. You're the only person can convince yourself of that.
JULIET	God knows I've tried, Freddie.
FREDDIE	Yeah, I think you have.
JULIET	These barriers ought not to exist.
FREDDIE	Sure, there ought to be no more wars, no religious intolerance, no race discrimination, no bombs — everyone in his right mind thinks that, and yet somehow, when we all get together, we find all these things are still there, and just a bit worse than before.
JULIET	(*with a trace of humour*) You're not very helpful.
FREDDIE	I know it.
JULIET	I don't know what's happened to you, Freddie. You've started to think.
FREDDIE	Sure. It was tough, but I made it.
JULIET	And you're a bit of a pessimist.
FREDDIE	(*with a vast smile*) Me, a pessimist? Not while there's baseball. Don't matter where I am, Paris, France, or this place, I have the scores phoned through to me every day.
JULIET	That's my boy.

FREDDIE	Yeah. One thing about baseball. It never lets you down.
JULIET	I'm sorry, dear.
FREDDIE	(*lightly*) That's Ok.
JULIET	(*after a pause*) D'you want to kiss me?
FREDDIE	No. I know when I'm licked.
JULIET	(*very upset*) Freddie!
FREDDIE	It wouldn't have worked, kid. You feel too strongly for me, know what I mean? I could never get as upset as you do, and that'd only upset me. I don't talk good, but you know what I mean. There'd be days with my great corny smile and the way I talk, well, it'd only irritate you. I really need a girl who doesn't want much out of life but what she sees . . . a girl who likes luxury but doesn't show it all the time . . . you see, I've got my problems too. Money's a hell of a thing to inherit. (*He rises.*) See you, Julie. Oh, I bought you some bangles off a guy in the street. I don't suppose you want them though.
JULIET	No, I don't . . . yes, give me them . . . they'll remind me of the dearest, sweetest guy I ever went with.
FREDDIE	I came out here with a brand new custom-made morning suit for my wedding . . . I'll go home alone . . . but remembered by a bangle . . . well, like I always say, that's life . . . I'll see you some place sometime . . . maybe you'll bring your husband over to see us . . . the kids can play in the pool.
JULIET	(*crying*) Don't, Freddie . . .
FREDDIE	God bless you, baby. Keep pitching.

(*He leaves her. She just stands, immobile.*)

BEULAH   That was the door, Hooper. Listen! They're both coming down the stairs. I can hear four feet.

MOULSWORTH   You'd better be right.

BEULAH   (*gentle*) Well, take that pioneering look off your face.

(MOULSWORTH *smiles with some difficulty. His smile vanishes much more easily as* FREDDIE *re-enters alone.*)

MOULSWORTH   Well?

FREDDIE   Well, I talked to her . . .

MOULSWORTH   We are waiting to hear what you said.

BEULAH   Freddie, what did she say?

FREDDIE   I don't know that we have a right to judge her.

MOULSWORTH   (*incredulous*) What was that?

FREDDIE   You see, sir . . . Mrs Moulsworth . . . I don't think I've ever seen anyone in love before.

BEULAH   Then it's real?

FREDDIE   Oh sure. Talking to her is about as hard as talking in church. Everything you say, why, you get a feeling you're interrupting, even when you're not. When I knew her, she was pretty. Now she's beautiful. I can't explain better than that.

BEULAH   (*her handkerchief to her cheek*) I know what you want to say, Freddie. I am a woman . . . and a mother. (*Suddenly surprised by the silence of her husband.*) Hooper?

MOULSWORTH	(*who has sat down heavily*) All the values of human conduct which I have learned to respect lie scattered around me. I just don't recognise anybody or anything any more. I'm just not fit to continue, that's all. I'm an old-timer, a has-been.
FREDDIE	Once again, sir . . . I guess that's life.
MOULSWORTH	(*snarling*) It's nothing of the sort, it's a goddamn disaster. Young man, there's no plane back to Miami until tomorrow morning. You're welcome to stay here, only keep out of my sight.
BEULAH	(*conciliatory*) Hooper . . .
MOULSWORTH	(*violent*) You too.
	(*The facade falls as the other rises. The other family is in session.* MARFA ZLOTOCHIENKO *is holding forth, and appears to be in full control.*)
MARFA	(*blonde and ferocious*) I shall be forced to report unfavourably on the state of this Embassy when I return. Your Secret Service man is in tears. No man who is in the habit of clouding his vision with tears can be consistently vigilant.
SPY	(*elated*) On then contrary, I am only just beginning to see! How can one understand our great and tortured history except through the magnifying glass of tears?
MARFA	Disgraceful. You, Comrade Ambassador, are guilty of indisputable apathy, and you, Comrade, who should be a mirror in which your husband can see his errors are but the distorting glass of the fun fair. As for your son — marriage is, of course, out of the question. It is totally unrealistic to embark on marriage with widowhood as imminent.

ROMANOFF	(*rising*) You can't mean what you are saying!
MARFA	What is the fate of the sleeping sentry? You are all asleep at your posts!
ROMANOFF	Evdokia! What has happened to you since we left Moscow?
EVDOKIA	We are traitors.
ROMANOFF	But why? Why? My son, you, me — is the rottenness in ourselves?
SPY	(*with staring, happy eyes*) I shall become a monk, that's what I will do — and place my tremendous capacity for patience at the disposal of meditation and the illumination of manuscripts.
ROMANOFF	There you are, it is contagious. Why?
EVDOKIA	If this means Siberia or death — I shall go out and buy that hat today — I have already telephoned the shop and asked them to reserve it for me — I must have a few hours of pleasure.
ROMANOFF	It must be this confounded country which is subversive — the climate — the atmosphere — (*To* MARFA.) Why do you look so sarcastic? You can know nothing about this country, you have only just arrived here.
MARFA	On the contrary, I am extremely well informed about it. conditions are chaotic, owing to a moribund economy. The atmosphere is one of sleepy indolence, and the climate is torrid in winter and more torrid in summer.
ROMANOFF	But . . . you have not lived through these summer nights.
MARFA	Summer nights? Of course I have, in the Black Sea. My eye never left the compass.

ROMANOFF	(*exasperated*) All your life you have seen nothing except that which met your eye, and you have noticed nothing except that which has been brought to your attention.
MARFA	Your insults do not affect me, Comrade. I am sure that I know more about this country than you do, in spite of your ambassadorial pretensions. What is the annual rainfall of the capital?
ROMANOFF	I haven't any idea, not do I think it affects the political situation.
MARFA	Three millimetres.
ROMANOFF	Thank you very much. I'm sure that the information will prove most valuable.
MARFA	And how many kilometres of narrow-gauge railroads are there?
ROMANOFF	I don't know. We walk.
MARFA	Six point seven, with another five which has been under construction since 1912. And how many secondary schools are there?
ROMANOFF	One.
MARFA	None.
ROMANOFF	Near enough.
MARFA	On the contrary. A hundred percent error. So don't tell me that I notice nothing but that which has been brought to my attention. I inform myself about everything, and as a consequence I am able to speak with authority. As for you, your Excellency, you are precisely the type of old-style foreign representative which honoured Artist K K Bolishkov attacked so brilliantly in his five act drama, "Kill the Swine."

ROMANOFF   A subtle title.

MARFA   You speak of subtlety as though it were a
            virtue.

ROMANOFF   It is a mark of intelligence. (*He studies
            her.*) Strange to have such a beautiful face,
            disfigured from the inside.

MARFA   Are you criticizing me?

ROMANOFF   We have a perfect right to criticize each
            other. It is a pastime enjoyed by the Party.
            You have been criticizing me since your
            arrival. Now its my turn. My criticism will
            take the form of a history lesson. Don't
            interrupt me — I am sure you know many
            more dates than I do, but I know more
            about our revolution than you do, because I
            was there! I remember the first glimmer of
            hope on a horizon which had been dead for
            years, no larger than a feather floating on
            the sea, but it was enough. I am not a
            religious man, but I used to go to church to
            hear the voices. There is no people which
            can sing as we can, and when the liberated
            passion of a thousand hearts streams into
            the golden dome, clashing, weaving,
            murmuring, roaring, then a man can
            believe in anything, for our battle cry is
            ecstasy. Some nations surpass themselves
            out of love, others out of hatred, others by
            contemplating the still waters of reason.
            We immortalize ourselves by ecstasy —
            and when the people saw that flicker of
            hope, they sang, millions of them, and
            made the sky more resonant than the
            cathedral roof. I saw expressions in the
            crowd which I shall never forget, the
            upturned eyes of dirty Byzantine angels,
            the smiles of women who believe in a truth
            so simple it defies description. The
            machine guns chattered in the cold,
            laughing victims fell painlessly to their

death, the snow was stained with blood.
Other voices took up the song, other feet
stepped forward, other hands grasped
home-made weapons. In the morning,
victory was ours, and many of the dead
were smiling still. Those were the days of
our enthusiasm. And what has happened
since? Our land has become a huge
laboratory, a palace of human test-tubes.
Our language, so rich, so masculine, so
muscular, is but a pale shadow of its
possibilities. Our literature, which ravished
the dark soul of man with such pity, is now
mobilized to serve an empty optimism. Our
music, divorced from sadness and the
twilight, has lost its anchor in an ocean of
dreariness. You my dear child, were born
into this monotonous nursery, and you have
never played with other toys than boredom,
pride and smugness. I blame you for
nothing. You know nothing. You are
nothing. And worse, you are no one. Do
with us what you will. I have rediscovered
my enthusiasm, and I will know how to
laugh, even in death.

EVDOKIA   (*emotional*) Vadim! We have a fine son!

(*Before the pale* MARFA *can say anything,*
EVDOKIA *and* VADIM *embrace with passion.*
MARFA *goes out.*)

SPY   (*with eyes sparkling*) Love must spread like
a plague . . . Oh God, save those who have
been immunized against emotion . . . help
those who marvel at figures of wheat
production, but who do not pause to marvel
at an ear of corn.

(MARFA *re-appears above.*)

MARFA   Lieutenant Romanoff!

IGOR   (*waking from his gloom*) Who are you?

MARFA	Junior Commander Marfa Vassilievna Zlotochienko.
IGOR	(*with a wan smile*) Oh, my wife. Are you blonde or brunette, thin or immensely fat?
MARFA	It is my duty to inform you that owing to the scandalous and anti-democratic attitude of your entire family, I will be forced to return by the first aeroplane tomorrow morning, and will further be forced to denounce the staff of this Embassy for anarchistic and fascist tendencies in surrendering to emotionalism of the most dangerous and subversive variety.
	(IGOR *starts laughing happily, almost hysterically.* MARFA *is taken aback, as though slapped in the face. The* PARENTS *break from their embrace, the* SPY *from his prayer.*)
EVDOKIA	(*gaily*) It's him laughing . . . Igor . . .
ROMANOFF	(*delighted*) Yes . . .
	(*They laugh. The* GENERAL *has re-appeared in the street and listens, surprised, as the front of the Embassy descends. The* SOLDIERS *stir. The light begins to lose its lustre. The* GENERAL *is dressed formally with top hat, gloves, a walking stick and a portfolio.*)
GENERAL	What a curious noise.
2ND SOLDIER	(*yawning*) It's the Russians laughing.
GENERAL	(*surprised*) Yes. Have you noticed anything? Has anyone entered or come out of the Embassies?
1ST SOLDIER	No, there's a seasonal slackness of business which lasts all the year round.
2ND SOLDIER	You're pretty warmly dressed for this weather, General.

GENERAL	(*weary*) It's not without reason that diplomats wear this kind of costume. Gloves, walking stick, portfolio, three articles to leave behind, if necessary.
1ST SOLDIER	Are you going in there?
GENERAL	I have been summoned to both Embassies at the same hour, and accepted both engagements in a fit of absent-mindedness. What is the time?
2ND SOLDIER	What's the use of asking us? There hasn't been a saint in sight for the past couple of hours. (*He looks at the clock.*) They must be having an argument in there.
1ST SOLDIER	Listen!

(*There is a hiss of machinery.* THREE SAINTS *appear very quickly, strike each other in confusion, and disappear at high speed.*)

That's called making up for lost time.

GENERAL	I came here with plenty of time in hand. Now I suddenly find myself in a desperate hurry. Men, I've had an idea. You remember this morning when Death made a mistake?
1ST SOLDIER 2ND SOLDIER }	Yes.
GENERAL	Why shouldn't Death really make a mistake? Wouldn't it be that our old friend up there was just dropping us a gentle hint? And isn't it possible that our Fatherland not only corrupts the living by making them oblivious of time, place, even of hatred — but that it makes even Death lazy and forgetful of his solemn duties? You don't follow. Human nature being what it is, legend and literature are full to overflowing with tragic lovers — there's

hardly a couple who don't end up
horizontal, bloody and fruitless. Why
should that be? What is the point of
suffering it you can't survive afterwards to
enjoy the relief.

2ND SOLDIER   I told you, if we weren't so weak, we could
threaten the two Governments responsible
for their unhappiness.

GENERAL   Don't make light of our weaknesses. These
days you have to be very, very strong to
allow yourself the luxury of being weak.

1ST SOLDIER   What do you suggest?

GENERAL   A trick! The prerogative of the weak.
Tonight we celebrate the Royal Marriage of
our Boy King Theodore the Uncanny to the
Infanta of Old Castille in 1311, which led
to the coalition of Saragossa, and the
eventual expulsion of the Albanians from
our soil.

2ND SOLDIER   Steady, sir, that's not til next Friday — and
you said this morning that is was the
Lithuanians who were driven out a
thousand years ago tonight.

GENERAL   Did I?

2ND SOLDIER   Yes.

GENERAL   Well, the great virtue of history is that it is
adaptable. I have a very definite reason for
wishing tonight to be the celebration of a
wedding, with the symbolic blessing of two
papier mache dummies by the Archbishop.
So shall we say that with the help of the
Spaniards we drove the Lithuanians out?

1ST SOLDIER   Doesn't sound very probable.

GENERAL   The pretext hardly matters. It's the
celebration which people enjoy.
Unfortunately even Easter has become

largely a matter of eggs. Now kindly
serenade the young lady with an apt folk
song . . . a melancholy one. Don't overdo it
. . . not tragic . . . just melancholy.

1st Soldier }   (*singing softly with guitar accompaniment*)
2nd Soldier   Oh, won't someone open the door of the cage
And set the bluebird free?
Set it free. Set it free.
It was caught in the spring at a tender age
It languished in summer, forgot how to sing
In the autumn it lost the use of one wing
Before winter comes and wild winds sting
Set it free. Set it free.
Set the bluebird free.

(Juliet *appears sadly and inquisitively on
her balcony.*)

JULIET   (*drab, with a little smile*) Oh, it's you.

GENERAL   Miss Moulsworth. Greetings. Listen to me.
It is extremely urgent. I need your help.

JULIET   You need *my* help?

GENERAL   Yes — If you wish to see the Lieutenant
again, you must do as I tell you.

JULIET   What do you want me to do?

GENERAL   Ssssh, not so loud. I want you to knot the
sheets of your bed, and to hang them from
your balcony.

JULIET   (*with some enthusiasm*) Like I did when I
ran away from school?

GENERAL   (*with excessive delight*) Did you? Yes.
(*Conspiratorial again.*) Then I want you to
write a farewell letter to your parents.

JULIET   What? Oh, I couldn't. As though I was
going to — no. Dad's got a weak heart.

GENERAL	You surprise me. Couch the letter in somewhat ambiguous terms. There's no need to mention the possibility of any rash act — just thank them for all they've done for you and say that you have run away to join the man you love.
JULIET	Even that might kill Dad.
GENERAL	The fact that you're happy?
JULIET	The fact that I didn't consult him first.
GENERAL	Really, I am running a little short of sympathy for him, Miss Moulsworth.
JULIET	He's a darling, really . . . at heart.
GENERAL	Must I doubt that you are really in love?
JULIET	(*hotly*) You've no right to doubt that, after what I've been through.
GENERAL	Then do as I tell you, and you will spread happiness round you like a cloak. You must trust me.
1ST SOLDIER	You must trust him!
2ND SOLDIER	Be a sport!
JULIET	(*doubtful*) Well . . .
GENERAL	It is a matter of life and death — for several people . . . don't let your parents go into old age with you on their conscience. It isn't fair. It isn't Christian.
JULIET	Yes, that's a thought. Ok, I'll do it.
GENERAL	You won't regret it.
	(JULIET *goes in.*)
1ST SOLDIER	What now?
GENERAL	Another folk song . . . something maritime . . . something about a sailor.

1ST SOLDIER 2ND SOLDIER }	Sailor where are you, are you? Is the storm on the sea? Is the storm in your heart? Which of these storms keeps up apart? Sailor where are you? are you? Are you faithless or dead Are the clouds in the sky? Are the clouds in your head? Sailor, my sailor, we'll never be wed. Sailor where are you . . .
	(IGOR *appears on his balcony, a haggard figure, holding a revolver.*)
IGOR	Why do you interrupt me?
GENERAL	Great heavens, Lieutenant Romanoff, what is that in your hand?
IGOR	A revolver, the classic solution to misery.
GENERAL	Are you aware that they are forbidden by law?
IGOR	How do you commit suicide then?
GENERAL	There are many other, less dangerous, methods.
IGOR	(*lifting it*) You're too late.
GENERAL	Lieutenant, you will see Juliet tonight.
IGOR	(*with a bitter laugh*) Really? Do you believe in the hereafter?
GENERAL	I believe in the herein.
IGOR	What is that?
GENERAL	Life as it is lived, with all its little annoyances.
IGOR	Little annoyances? You have never suffered.

GENERAL	No, and I don't intend to. Lieutenant, do something for me before you die.
IGOR	What?
GENERAL	Write a farewell letter to your parents.
IGOR	I have already done so. It covers seventeen pages. Then I ran out of ink.
GENERAL	And Lieutenant, will you tie the sheets of your bed together, and then fix them to the balcony?
IGOR	As though I were running away?
GENERAL	Yes — No! As though you were advancing to happiness.
IGOR	I am an officer, sir. I am incapable of cowardice.
GENERAL	I understand your prejudice, sir since, believe it or not, I am an officer myself. I am incapable of almost everything, but at the moment I do happen to know what I am talking about. If you wish to see Juliet again, alive, well, happy, do as I tell you. Give me a startling demonstration of seaman's knots.
IGOR	I cannot. My mind is made up.
	(The SPY *sidles out of the Embassy, then rushes up to the* GENERAL.)
GENERAL	(*horrified*) What do you want?
SPY	(*desperate*) I am on your side. Help me, and I will help you.
GENERAL	What do you want?
SPY	Asylum.
GENERAL	Granted.

Spy	And —
General	What?
Spy	A letter of introduction to the most austere, the most rigid and terrible monastery in your country.
General	We will send you to the Mauve Friars. They never sit or stand. They walk about on their knees.
Spy	(*grasping the* General's *hand and kissing it rapturously*) Oh, exquisite. My eternal gratitude.

(Igor *is about to shoot. The* General *sees this.*) |
General	Quick!
Spy	"Last night we were as one, creatures in a dream, selflessly united in an endless waltz. From now on we are opposed, a man and a woman in love, the greatest, most exhausting struggle in the world, two moths racing for the flame, two cannibals devouring each other."
Igor	(*limp, he lets the revolver drop with a clatter*) Farewell, resolution. How did you remember that?
Spy	I listened in the shadows, and took it down in shorthand. Then as I read it in my room at night, I began to feel lonely again, and jealous that such phrases should not have been addressed to me.
Igor	Jealous? Am I capable of inspiring jealousy? Even in my present condition?
Spy	Oh yes, brother . . . yes . . . your life is still before you, even if it only lasts ten minutes . . . while I must expiate my sins in endless penances and terrifying disciplines.

IGOR	(*with a little sigh of relief*) What a fool I am . . . we must rely on one another to understand ourselves. What did you want? Ah yes. Sheets. Is it for some joke?
GENERAL	Yes, yes, a joke.
IGOR	I like jokes. (*He goes.*)
SPY	Now — your part of the bargain.
GENERAL	Boys, take this gentleman to my office. I'll be along presently.
SPY	I'd rather wait in church if I may.
1ST SOLDIER	(*in disgust*) Church?
GENERAL	Well I'll find out in which establishment the bread is hardest, the water dirtiest, and liqueur least potent.
SPY	Thank you, thank you.
	(*As the* TWO SOLDIERS *go, both facades rise.* HOOPER MOULSWORTH *is alone and consults his watch. In the other Embassy,* VADIM ROMANOFF *is also alone, and also consults his watch. Both seem exasperated. Upstairs,* JULIET *is writing a letter, and choosing her words carefully, while* IGOR *is tying his sheets in complicated knots. The* GENERAL *enters the American Embassy.*)
GENERAL	(*beaming*) Not too early, I trust?
MOULSWORTH	I make you just on two hours late, but then I don't know the time around here any more than anyone else does. As it happens, it's not important as my Washington call seems to be delayed. Cigar?
GENERAL	Thank you.
MOULSWORTH	Now, let's come straight to the point. I talk blunt. When I want to know something, I just ask. That's the way I operate.

GENERAL   I appreciate that. In my position, I have to
                    appreciate almost everything.

MOULSWORTH   Are you or are you not going to come into
                    the Western community? I've got to know
                    right now.

GENERAL   And how is your charming daughter?

MOULSWORTH   What's that? She's just fine, thanks. Just
                    fine. Now if you're not going to play ball
                    with us, just who are you going to play ball
                    with, and why?

GENERAL   Yes. She looked exquisite last night, I thought.

MOULSWORTH   Who?

GENERAL   Your daughter.

MOULSWORTH   Didn't she though? Now look, no nation
                    can afford to remain neutral these days, not
                    with the bomb and economic pressures.

GENERAL   Who was that attractive young man she was
                    with?

MOULSWORTH   (*livid*) Leave him out of this.

GENERAL   Her fiance, perhaps? Will we soon hear the
                    bells?

MOULSWORTH   No!

                    (*The telephone rings.*)

                    Oh, damn it! Excuse me. I thought I told
                    you I didn't want to be interrupted . . .
                    Who? (*Different voice.*) Washington?
                    (*Ingratiating.*) Mr President . . . ? Oh,
                    she's just fine, thanks . . . sure, she's fine
                    too . . . Sure and she's fine too . . . I hope
                    to have them wrapped up and in the
                    Western community by nightfall . . . Oh,
                    sure, I've pointed that out . . . They've got

a lot of pretty old-fashioned ideas . . . No
sir, I can't talk too freely right now . . .
That's it, sir, that's the situation . . . Right
here with me . . . Yeah, I'll do that, he'll
appreciate it . . .

(*The* SOVIET AMBASSADOR *manifests
considerable impatience in his room.*)

Yeah . . . No, I don't need anything, sir . . .
I'd be grateful if you could tell me the time
though, sir. Then I'd add six hours and
fifty minutes, and know what time it is here
. . . Is that right? Why, thank you, sir . . .
(*He adjusts his watch while talking.*) Ok,
sir, yes . . . And our fondest personal
regards to Mrs President . . . Goodbye . . .
(*With a sudden burst of laughter.*) Sure I
remember the time . . . When I fell in the
swimming pool with all my clothes on . . .
Sure, sure . . . had a hell of a lot of laughs
. . . Goodbye . . . (*He hangs up.*) Great guy.
Hey, you know something . . . you were two
hours and forty six minutes late.

GENERAL   And I thought I was ten minutes early.

MOULSWORTH   What were we talking about? Oh, before I
                 forget it, Mr President sends his warmest
                 good wishes for the financial prosperity of
                 your nation.

GENERAL   Thank you sir. And when you next
                 telephone him, would you express to him
                 my warmest good wishes for the financial
                 prosperity of your nation.

MOULSWORTH   (*no longer interested*) Sure. Thanks. Now —

GENERAL   We were talking about your daughter.

MOULSWORTH   We were? Hey, you noticed nothing . . .
                 nothing strange last night, did you?

GENERAL   With your daughter?

MOULSWORTH	Yes. Nothing . . . visibly . . . untoward?
GENERAL	No, except that she seemed radiantly happy.
MOULSWORTH	(*weary*) Don't tell me, don't tell me. Those facts I don't retain. It's certainly a pretty exhausting life you lead us diplomats. Always celebrating, never an evening at home. (*Suddenly firm.*) We were going to discuss the Western community, weren't we, before you side-tracked me?
GENERAL	Not now, Your Excellency. You have pointed out yourself that it's very much later than we thought. I have to open a bridge half an hour ago.
MOULSWORTH	(*very energetic*) I must have your answer tonight.
GENERAL	(*elegant*) Perhaps we could find a moment to talk during the celebration?
MOULSWORTH	Celebration?
GENERAL	Yes, the Russians will accept, I feel sure.
MOULSWORTH	Another Independence Day?
GENERAL	Yes. Two as it happens. (*Awkward pause. Then suddenly.*) Goodbye.
	(*He goes, leaving his portfolio and his gloves, and crosses swiftly to the Russian Embassy. The* US AMBASSADOR *finds the articles, makes to follow, then throws them down, and pours himself a whisky. The* GENERAL *enters the Russian Embassy.*)
	Not too early, I trust?
ROMANOFF	Only if I misunderstood the appointment, and it was for tomorrow.
GENERAL	(*laughing*) I apologise.

(MARFA *enters*.)

ROMANOFF   What is it?

MARFA   Good afternoon.

GENERAL   (*surveying her*) Good afternoon.

MARFA   Because of the defection of your habitual
                cipher-clerk, I have intercepted the
                message.

ROMANOFF   (*takes a typewritten document*) Thank you.

                (MARFA *goes*.)

                Please excuse me.

GENERAL   Yes, of course.

ROMANOFF   (*he reads quickly*) Now, I am directed to
                enquire of you whether or not you have
                finally decided to adhere to the Eastern Bloc.

GENERAL   How is your charming son?

ROMANOFF   (*abrupt*) Not well. He will be leaving soon.
                It is imperative that we know by tonight.

GENERAL   He seemed to be throwing himself into the
                spirit of our national carnival.

ROMANOFF   It is a temptation which all of us must resist.

GENERAL   Otherwise you might become like us?

ROMANOFF   A sense of humour sabotages industrial
                development.

GENERAL   (*laughs — then realizes that a joke was not
                intended*) He was with a very beautiful girl
                last night.

ROMANOFF   Please stick to the point. (*He consults the
                document.*) I see that the President himself
                has asked for your co-operation. I quote,
                "At any price", unquote.

GENERAL	(*incredulous*) You know more than I do.
ROMANOFF	You must know that we tap your wires.
GENERAL	I know you do, but we don't. I always find a keyhole an unsatisfactory frame.
ROMANOFF	It depends on your possibilities. Once we have taken the trouble to penetrate their codes, it is a pity not to benefit from the results.
GENERAL	Quite. It's like acquiring a degree, and then not practising. (*He rises.*) I hope to see you at our little celebration tonight.
ROMANOFF	My wife is very tired . . . so am I . . .
GENERAL	The Americans have accepted.
ROMANOFF	(*with a deep sigh*) We will be there.
GENERAL	Goodbye, sir.
ROMANOFF	Goodbye,
	(*He leaves — without his walking stick. He crosses to the American Embassy. The* SOVIET AMBASSADOR *finds the stick, puts it down absently, and pours himself vodka. The* GENERAL *appears in the American Embassy.*)
GENERAL	(*genial*) I find I left my portfolio.
MOULSWORTH	And your gloves.
GENERAL	Those are not my gloves.
MOULSWORTH	No?
GENERAL	No.
MOULSWORTH	Oh. Drink?
GENERAL	No, thank you.
MOULSWORTH	Cigar?

GENERAL	Thank you. Incidentally, they know your code.
MOULSWORTH	(*beaming*) We know they know our code.
GENERAL	Oh, really.
MOULSWORTH	Sure. We only give them things we want them to know.
GENERAL	(*after a very long pause in which the* GENERAL *tries to make head or tail of this intelligence*) Goodbye.
MOULSWORTH	See you. *And make up your mind!*
	(*The* GENERAL *leaves as the* US AMBASSADOR *chuckles with pleasure. The* GENERAL *crosses to the Russian Embassy.*)
GENERAL	I think I forgot my walking stick.
ROMANOFF	Here it is.
GENERAL	Incidentally, they know you know their code.
ROMANOFF	(*laughing*) That does not surprise me in the least. We have known for some time that they knew we knew their code. We have acted accordingly — by pretending to be duped.
GENERAL	(*after another incredulous pause*) I never realized how simple my life was.
ROMANOFF	Remember. Tonight is the deadline.
GENERAL	Goodbye.
	(*He leaves and crosses to the American Embassy.* ROMANOFF *sits sadly. Pause. The* GENERAL *enters the American Embassy.*)
MOULSWORTH	Oh. Come right in. So you've come to sign, heh?

| GENERAL | Not yet. I find on investigation that those gloves were mine after all. |

| MOULSWORTH | I thought they were. This life seems to be getting you down. Cigar? |

| GENERAL | Thank you. Incidentally, they know you know they know you know the code. |

| MOULSWORTH | (*genuinely alarmed*) What? Are you sure? |

| GENERAL | I'm positive. |

| MOULSWORTH | (*hearty*) Thanks. I shan't forget this. |

| GENERAL | (*amused*) You mean you didn't know? |

| MOULSWORTH | No! |

| GENERAL | (*his majesty restored*) Goodbye. |

| MOULSWORTH | You haven't left anything? |

| GENERAL | No. Goodbye. |

(*He goes and meets the* TWO SOLDIERS.)

| 1ST SOLDIER | We had to leave him in the church. We go on guard in half an hour. |

| GENERAL | I could do with a quick prayer myself. Cigar? |

(*He puts one in his own mouth. All three light up and tiptoe out as* IGOR *and* JULIET *begin to let their sheets over the balcony. They see each other.*)

| JULIET | Igor! |

| IGOR | Juliet? |

(*As their hands reach ineffectually for each other, the curtain falls.*)

ACT THREE

Evening to night.

It is evening, and the stage presents a scene of imminent enchantment. The street lamps are lit, and an elaborate gilt altar-piece has been erected in the available space between the two Embassies. It is evidently of considerable age, and its spiral columns of tawny gold are lit by a host of candles. There are flags here and there. In the distance, music, music for the open air, brass instruments and the murmur of people.

The TWO SOLDIERS *enter, in their uniforms, now more formal in appearance. They carry two life-size papier-mache figures of the type used in religious celebrations. They have doll-like faces, staring eyes, and are evidently either of great antiquity or else made by most spontaneous and artistic peasant craftsmen. The front view of these figures, one male, one female, have a weather-beaten beauty, and are picked out in drab and subtle colours. On their backs, however, are attached priceless robes of a former age, their magnificence enhanced by their oldness. The* GENERAL *follows the* TWO SOLDIERS *on. He is dressed in a uniform which hovers between the exquisite and the ludicrous. Plumes, swords, spurs, the whole works.*

1ST SOLDIER   Where d'you want them?

GENERAL   Here will do. (*He mops his brow.*)
        Everything in place? The sheets? Yes. The
        letters? Attached to the sheets. Splendid.
        There's so much to talk about.

2ND SOLDIER   The Archbishop didn't seem very pleased at
        your suggestion, General.

GENERAL   A deaf Archbishop can be a nuisance, but
        tonight he may have his advantages. Of
        course, he only became Archbishop because
        he is entirely closed to the world of sound.
        It gave him an austerity which visibly
        enhanced his capacity for meditation.

1ST SOLDIER   Look out. Here he is.

GENERAL   (*irritated*) He mustn't come here! We don't
                   want to have to start shouting under the
                   very walls of the Embassies.

                   (*But the* ARCHBISHOP, *who is at least 100
                   years old and very small, approaches with
                   a royal and terrible step. His train, which
                   is of extreme length, and his mitre, which
                   is of extreme weight, are being supported
                   by our friend the* SPY, *now dressed in
                   mauve rags, his head practically entirely
                   occupied by an enormous tonsure, his eye
                   brilliant with ecstasy.*)

                   (*ingratiating*) My Lord Archbishop.

ARCHBISHOP   (*who has a querulous but frightening voice*)
                   General, this is an outrage! I have
                   consulted many Holy books, and I find
                   what I had indeed suspected, that the
                   celebration of that most Royal Marriage
                   between the Boy King Theodore the
                   Uncanny and the Infanta of Old Bastille
                   does not fall until next Friday, and that
                   tonight we celebrate our heroic
                   participation in the Children's Crusade so
                   kindly have these invaluable symbols
                   transported back to the National Museum
                   with all despatch.

GENERAL   (*very loud*) Today is Friday.

ARCHBISHOP   Kindly stop mumbling.

GENERAL   (*shouting*) Today is Friday.

ARCHBISHOP   You must speak up more.

GENERAL   (*softly, to the audience*) I surrender. I tell
                   him today is Friday, and —

ARCHBISHOP   Today Friday? Nonsense. Today is
                   Wednesday the fourteenth. It has been
                   since midnight.

GENERAL   (*recovering from the shock — very, very softly*) Can you hear me now?

ARCHBISHOP   (*irritated*) Of course I can hear you. If people wouldn't mumble so, I could hear everything.

GENERAL   (*soft*) It's all the fault of the clock of St Ambrose.

ARCHBISHOP   What's wrong with the clock of St Ambrose?

GENERAL   Since it was built it has been losing time.

ARCHBISHOP   Losing time?

GENERAL   (*normal*) Yes.

ARCHBISHOP   Mumbling again!

GENERAL   (*very soft*) I beg your pardon. Yes. It has been computed by our Academy of Sciences that since thirteen eleven it has lost precisely two days.

ARCHBISHOP   The clock was not built in thirteen eleven.

GENERAL   It would have lost two days had it been built in thirteen eleven.

ARCHBISHOP   Gracious. Then it's Friday today.

GENERAL   Exactly.

ARCHBISHOP   Then we are not celebrating our contribution to the Children's Crusade at all.

GENERAL   No, we aren't.

ARCHBISHOP   What are we celebrating then?

GENERAL   The marriage of the Boy King Theodore the Uncanny and the Infanta of Old Castille.

ARCHBISHOP   (*joining in*) Infanta of Old Castille. We shall then need the traditional altar of St

Boleslav and the religious figures of the
young couple for the symbolic wedding.

GENERAL   They are already in place. Now, if I may
refresh your memory, Your Altitude . . .

(GENERAL *re-directs* ARCHBISHOP'S *attention
to Altar and the two figures.*)

ARCHBISHOP   (*sees them*) My, my, how thoughtful of you.
Verily, we have an efficient President at last.

GENERAL   (*with some amusement*) I see, my Lord
Archbishop, that you are well satisfied with
the new convert I sent you.

ARCHBISHOP   To whom are you referring?

GENERAL   The Mauve Friar at your heels.

(*The* ARCHBISHOP *extends his hands with a
smile. The* SPY *comes forward on his knees
and is patted on his bald head, which he
finds an elevating experience.*)

ARCHBISHOP   He was admitted into the Holy Unorthodox
Church an hour ago, and was the only one
to volunteer to carry my mitre, which is of
crushing weight, and my train, which is of
transcendent volume, on this great
occasion. It is disgraceful how lazy we are
as a nation. Mark my words, he will go a
long way. Maybe, when I am gone —

SPY   No, no, no . . .

ARCHBISHOP   He has been absolved for one day from his
vow of silence, as he will help me with the
ritual. Owing to my extreme age, my
memory has failed me, thank God, before
my heart or mind. I will prepare for the
solemnities.

(*The* GENERAL *and the* TWO SOLDIERS *bow as
the* ARCHBISHOP *leaves with the
overburdened* SPY.)

2ND SOLDIER	Even if one doesn't approve of your politics one has to admire you.
1ST SOLDIER	I suppose so. (*He spits.*)
	(*The facades of both Embassies rise. The* US AMBASSADOR, *in full tenue, enters. He is having difficulty with his tie.* BEULAH *follows in a violet evening dress. The upstairs rooms are empty.*)
BEULAH	I can't help you with your tie, Hooper, if you won't stay still.
MOULSWORTH	I'm nervous. I've taken twelve vitamin pills and I'm still nervous. How do you like that?
BEULAH	(*working on his tie*) I wish we didn't have to go.
MOULSWORTH	For the thousandth time, Beulah, we just have to go. A doctor is always on call. So's a diplomat. That pact has just got to be signed tonight.
BEULAH	I never realized this country was so important.
MOULSWORTH	A casting vote is the important vote in any board meeting. Where's Freddie?
BEULAH	He went out a lot earlier.
MOULSWORTH	What to do?
BEULAH	(*blank*) Have some fun, he said.
MOULSWORTH	Fun. I'm glad he's not marrying Julie. Positively glad. Have you finished?
BEULAH	Stand still.
MOULSWORTH	Has Julie eaten?

BEULAH	I put a tray by her door, but she just didn't answer.
MOULSWORTH	Goddamn it, Beulah, you're heavy-handed.
	(*The* RUSSIAN COUPLE *enter.*)
ROMANOFF	Evdokia, I asked you to help me with my tie.
EVDOKIA	Come here, into the light.
ROMANOFF	Where is that odious Comrade Zlotochienko? Every room I go into I expect to find her there, tapping wires or thumbing her way through my papers.
EVDOKIA	She went out to do a social survey of living conditions here. She wants to lecture her crew when she gets home.
ROMANOFF	I don't envy them. And Igor? Has he eaten?
EVDOKIA	The loaf of bread I left by his door has not been touched. I knocked, but he was sulking.
ROMANOFF	Ow!
EVDOKIA	I'm sorry. I'm tired. I wish we didn't have to go.
ROMANOFF	It's my last manoeuvre for Moscow. I might as well do it properly. Why do you look so sad?
EVDOKIA	I shall never be a grandmother.
BEULAH	There.
MOULSWORTH	Yeah. Feels good. Well. Time for a drink?
BEULAH	Hooper, you'd better not. Not after all those pills. Not if you have to sign a treaty.
MOULSWORTH	Guess you're right. Well. Got everything?
EVDOKIA	Finished.
ROMANOFF	Thank you. Now, shut your eyes.

EVDOKIA	What?
ROMANOFF	Shut your eyes, and don't turn round.
EVDOKIA	(*resigned*) Are you going to shoot me?
ROMANOFF	We'll think of that tomorrow. (*He produces her beloved hat from a small box, and puts it gently on her head.*) You may open your eyes.
EVDOKIA	(*whose fingers are feeling her head, with a shriek of joy*) Vadim! The hat! (*They embrace.*) How could you?
ROMANOFF	I left and came back by the tradesmen's entrance.
EVDOKIA	Oh, Vadim.
ROMANOFF	There. Let us go.
EVDOKIA	One more kiss.
MOULSWORTH	(*about to exit*) I've been thinking, Beulah.
BEULAH	Yes, Hooper?
MOULSWORTH	How about a real good holiday soon? Just the two of us, like it was our honeymoon.
BEULAH	Hooper, d'you mean that?
MOULSWORTH	Never meant anything more sincerely in my life. (*They kiss, too. As they do, the Embassies close. The* GENERAL *marches up and takes his position centre stage. The doors of both Embassies open, and both couples emerge at the same time. They bow coldly.*)
GENERAL	Ah! How nice to see you here. The formal part of the celebrations are about to begin. Then afterwards we abandon ourselves to more profane pleasures.

1ST SOLDIER	Regiment. Present — arms!
GENERAL	(*sotto-voice*) Quite smart, but a little late. Try to remember next year . . . (*Loud again.*) Now, maybe a short historical resume of the character of this Thanksgiving will not be entirely out of place. If you can find us on the map, and there are many, alas, who cannot, you will see at once that our position, geographically, militarily, financially, politically, administratively, economically, agriculturally, horticulturally, is quite hopeless. Consequently we have acted as a magnet to the invader throughout our long and troubled history. The English have been here on several occasions on the pretext that we were unfit to govern ourselves. They were invariably followed by the French on the pretext that we were unfit to be governed by the English. The Dutch made us Protestants for a while, the Turks made us Mohammedans, the Italians made us . . . sing quite beautifully . . . and these many centuries in close proximity to homesick and miserable soldiers has brought quick maturity to our men and babies of all colours to our women . . . The year 1311 was not a particularly eventful one in our history . . . apart from the fact that the Albanians and the Lithuanians were both casting envious eyes on our territory at the same time, which rendered our traditional policy of balance of feebleness impractical. There was in fact an unwritten treaty between these two powers to split our land between them. The treaty was unwritten because at that period in history neither the Albanians nor the Lithuanians could write. The situation was further aggravated by the assassination of our Emperor, Thomas the Impossible, by an Albanian desperado disguised as a bunch of

flowers. However, our Boy King came to our rescue and contracted a rapid Spanish marriage which brought Spanish troops to our assistance on condition we became Catholic. We did for a while until the Albanians and Lithuanians decimated each other when we reverted yet again to the Holy Unorthodox Religion of our forefathers. It is this subtle trick which we celebrate today with much pomp and majesty. These are the symbolic figures, this of Theodore 1310-1311, Boy King. And this of Inez, the Infanta of Old Castille.

BEULAH   Isn't that interesting. I just adore history. It's so old.

MOULSWORTH   I wish there was some place to sit.

GENERAL   Ah! Silence please. The gentlemen will remove their hats.

                (*The* ARCHBISHOP *enters and stands before the Altar. The* SPY *follows on his knees, and squats by his side.*)

EVDOKIA   By all that's holy! Do you see what I see, Vadim?

ROMANOFF   (*unsurprised*) With him you can never tell if he's not still engaged in his old profession.

MOULSWORTH   Ssssh!

ARCHBISHOP   We are gathered here to observe in great solemnity the matrimony which saved our land on one of, alas, numerous occasions, from the savage heel of the invader. People of our country! Great powers to the east and to the west gird up their loins for war. Their regiments abound with Goliaths. We have only one David with which to oppose them — the Boy King Theodore the Eighth.

He, in his wisdom and uncanniness, begs
for the hand of Inez, the Infanta of . . . (*He
dries up.*)

SPY   (*softly*) Old Castille.

ARCHBISHOP   Old Castille. She accepts. The marriage
which saved our fatherland is celebrated
again. The tapestry of history unfurls. Let
us . . . (*He dries up.*)

SPY   (*consulting a document, softly*) Remember . . .

ARCHBISHOP   Remember the days of our distress. The
bells are silent, the soil untilled, the fields
barren . . . (*He dries up.*) What now?

SPY   (*softly*) Come forth . . .

ARCHBISHOP   Oh yes. Come forth, Theodore Alaric
Demetrius Pompey, by the Will of the
People Most Divine Protector of the
Unwilling, Mentor of the Undecided,
Emperor Absolute and Undisputed. Come
forth, Inez Dolores Chiquita Amparo
Conchita Concepcion Maria, Infanta
Extraordinary of Old Castille, Hereditary
Inheritor of Splendour, Purveyor of
Wisdom, Holder of the Keys of Pamplona.

(*The* SOLDIERS *carry forward the figures and
place them before the* ARCHBISHOP, *with
their backs to the audience. Their absence
from their original positions now reveals
the sheets hanging from the balconies.*)

BEULAH   (*with a shriek*) Hooper! Julie's window! It's
open.

MOULSWORTH   She's gone!

EVDOKIA   Vadim, the balcony!

ROMANOFF   He has escaped!

EVDOKIA   He's left a message!

BEULAH	She's left a message!
GENERAL	A little quiet please. This is the most solemn part of the ceremony.
MOULSWORTH	(*furious*) You must have known about this — why didn't you tell us?
GENERAL	(*pointedly*) We never interfere in the affairs of other nations.
ROMANOFF	You mean you left these sheets dangling from our balconies for everyone to see?
GENERAL	Very few people pass by here. Now, silence, please!
ARCHBISHOP	The marriage will now be solemnized.
BEULAH	(*who has read the message, howling*) Julie! She's gone, Hooper! Gone to find her happiness with . . . with *him*.
MOULSWORTH	(*furious, to* ROMANOFF) You had a hand in this. (*To the* GENERAL.) I'll get you for this. I'll declare war. My only daughter.
EVDOKIA	(*a scream*) Vadim . . . he speaks of suicide . . . life no longer holds anything without love or dialectic . . . wishes to die.
ROMANOFF	(*frantic, to* MOULSWORTH) It's all the fault of your confounded daughter. My son, my son.
	(*He kneels and weeps.* EVDOKIA *throws herself on him. During this the* ARCHBISHOP *has been muttering.*)
MOULSWORTH	I . . . I . . .
BEULAH	(*screeching*) Hooper. *Do* something!
MOULSWORTH	Stop that man from talking first!
GENERAL	(*loud*) The Archbishop is stone deaf.

ARCHBISHOP	Do you, Theodore Alaric —
MOULSWORTH	I'll get my car —
ARCHBISHOP	Demetrius Pompey —
MOULSWORTH	Search every — have the frontier sealed.
GENERAL	(*indulgent*) Quiet, please!
ARCHBISHOP	By the Will of the People —
MOULSWORTH	Let me see that note.
BEULAH	(*desperate*) It has no forwarding address.
ARCHBISHOP	Most Divine Protector of the Unwilling —
MOULSWORTH	I'll call Washington.
ARCHBISHOP	Mentor of the Undecided.
MOULSWORTH	(*to* GENERAL, *fuming*) Call out the police!
ARCHBISHOP	Emperor Absolute and Undisputed . . . (*He dries up.*) Yes?
SPY	Alias Igor Vadimovitch Romanoff.
MOULSWORTH	Hey, those figures have shrunk!
ARCHBISHOP	Alias Igor Vadimovitch Romanoff.
ROMANOFF	Igor!
ARCHBISHOP	Take this woman to be your lawfully wedded wife?
IGOR	(*dressed in robes*) I do.
ARCHBISHOP	Do you, Inez Dolores —
MOULSWORTH	Stop the ceremony! It's a trick!
	(*The* SOLDIERS *bar the passage with their rifles.*)
ARCHBISHOP	Chiquita Amparo —
ROMANOFF	Stop! Stop! Stop!
EVDOKIA	Vadim, why?

ARCHBISHOP	Conchita Concepcion —
MOULSWORTH	(*to the* GENERAL) I'll have you bombed . . . I'll summon the United Nations.
ARCHBISHOP	Maria, Infanta of Old Castille —
BEULAH	My girl, my girl.
ROMANOFF	We are impotent.
ARCHBISHOP	Hereditary Inheritor of Splendour.
MOULSWORTH	This calls for concerted action.
ROMANOFF	We have not the habit of collaboration.
ARCHBISHOP	Purveyor of Wisdom.
MOULSWORTH	(*to* GENERAL) You have threatened the United States Ambassador —
ARCHBISHOP	Holder of the Keys of Pamplona . . . (*He dries up.*) Yes?
SPY	Alias Juliet Alison Murphy Vanderwelde Moulsworth.
ARCHBISHOP	Alias Juliet alison Murphy Vanderwelde Moulsworth . . . I don't remember that in the ritual.
MOULSWORTH	(*shouting*) Sure you don't! I said, sure you don't!
SPY	It is here, in illuminated letters of the fourteenth century.
ARCHBISHOP	Then it must be my memory again. Do you take this man as your lawfully wedded husband?
MOULSWORTH	No!
JULIET	Yes.
	(BEULAH *needs comforting — so does* EVDOKIA.)

ARCHBISHOP   I hereby pronounce you man and wife. Kiss
                    your wife.

                    (IGOR *does so.*)

                    He is surprisingly mobile for a papier-
                    mache figure. Place the ring on her finger.
                    Now go out there, my son, and beat the
                    Albanians. Let the bells ring.

                    (*The bells ring. A great shout of triumph
                    rises from the populace. Fireworks begin to
                    crackle. The married couple, who had
                    substituted themselves for the wax figures
                    during the discovery of the sheets, turn
                    towards us, radiantly happy.*)

                    A miracle! Oh, well. That's quite unusual.

                    (*The* ARCHBISHOP *and the* SPY *leave, the* SPY
                    triumphant and laughing.)

MOULSWORTH   It's not valid under American law.

ROMANOFF   It will not be recognized in the Soviet Union.

EVDOKIA   But Vadim — to see our son so happy!

IGOR   Father. Mother. May I present — ?

JULIET   Dad. Mom. I want you to know —

                    (*The* US AMBASSADOR *and* SOVIET
                    AMBASSADOR *turn their backs. Shyly,*
                    BEULAH *and* EVDOKIA *look at each other.*)

BEULAH   Why, Mrs Romanoff . . .

EVDOKIA   (*emotional*) Comrade Moulsworth . . . What
                    are we to do? Isn't it always left to the
                    women to make peace?

BEULAH   Why, yes, to see our children so happy . . .

MOULSWORTH   (*sharply*) Beulah, I refuse to let you listen
                    to that woman's peace feelers.

ROMANOFF	(*sharply*) Evdokia, whatever you may have said and felt, we are Russian. You are walking into a capitalist trap.
	(*A pause of indecision.*)
BEULAH	(*precipitately*) Julie.
JULIET	Mother.
	(*They embrace.*)
BEULAH	May I kiss Igor, and welcome him into our family?
IGOR	My second mother.
	(*They kiss.*)
EVDOKIA	Igor!
IGOR	Mamasha!
EVDOKIA	And now let my welcome my new daughter.
JULIET	Oh, Mrs Romanoff . . .
	(*They kiss.*)
MOULSWORTH	(*who is dying to turn around*) Beulah, I shall not forget this. Your foolishness has cost me my job, my dignity, and my self-respect.
BEULAH	Hooper, darling, don't be so silly.
MOULSWORTH	You are condoning the actions of a government which has threatened your husband with loaded rifles.
GENERAL	Loaded? Only with blanks.
ROMANOFF	What?
GENERAL	Regiment. Into the air. Fire!
	(*Two mild little shots, like caps.*)
	Good.

MOULSWORTH	D'you mean to tell me . . . ?
GENERAL	(*smiling*) We could only have acquired live ammunition by joining either the Western Community or the Eastern Bloc. We manufacture none ourselves.
JULIET	(*appealing*) Pop.
IGOR	(*appealing*) Pappa.
	(*Pause. In a rush, the fathers embrace their children.*)
GENERAL	(*triumphant*) From now on, we will no longer celebrate the marriage of our Boy King . . . let the effigies rest in peace in the museum . . . the Lithuanians and Albanians no longer threaten anyone . . . like us, they cling to existence with the claws of hope . . . from now on and into the future, we will celebrate this, our greatest victory . . . every year . . . on the right day . . . at the right hour . . .
ROMANOFF	(*suddenly*) Tell me . . . why am I not unhappy? By the rules of prejudice, I should be overwhelmed with bitterness.
IGOR	You are not unhappy because I am happy, father . . . and because we're in a happy country . . .
ROMANOFF	I need proof of that. Happy? It can't be happy without a single factory, without a collective farm, without a communal centre.
1ST SOLDIER	I thought like that, too, Your Excellency — but tonight. I wonder . . .
MOULSWORTH	I don't get it, either, now we're talking about it. I ought to be just thunderstruck, just right in the throes of a breakdown, and yet I feel as though . . . as though I'd just had a shower in champagne. (*He kisses his daughter.*) What's your subsoil like?

GENERAL	(*pleasantly*) I haven't the slightest idea.
MOULSWORTH	(*investigating the ground*) I bet it's lousy with oil.
GENERAL	(*violently*) Then kindly leave it where it is. We only need to strike oil in order to be invaded tomorrow.
MOULSWORTH	Hey, some philosophy. Will you get that? A guy who doesn't want to own a Cadillac, on account of it's bound to be stolen.
JULIET	It makes sense to me, Pop.
MOULSWORTH	(*laughing*) Already? You've been here too long.
BEULAH	May I compliment you on your hat, madame?
EVDOKIA	(*blushing*) Thank you.
BEULAH	It's just darling.
ROMANOFF	I still need proof that I am legitimately happy —
IGOR	(*amused*) Father, you're so didactic.
ROMANOFF	(*severely*) So were you, yesterday. If we are to stay here — and obviously we cannot return to Moscow with any degree of safety — then I must know why I am so happy. Is it owing to a deeply frivolous nature, or is there something strangely, yet pleasantly, subversive in the very atmosphere of this place?
GENERAL	Ah, he's getting warmer. Isn't he, men?
2ND SOLDIER	(*with a sigh*) Yes, he is. It's in the air . . .
MOULSWORTH	Yeah. We can't return home either, Beulah. What can we tell the neighbours? So, we'll have to stay here for a while. But somehow — can't put my finger on the reason — but

right now, I don't care. I don't care who signs which treaty with who. It's all way behind me — or maybe, it's way below me.

ROMANOFF   Yes — but speaking personally, I must know the cause. I must have proof.

(*The* SPY *runs conspiratorially round the corner.*)

SPY   Proof?

ROMANOFF   Have you been listening?

SPY   That is one habit I can never lose. If you want proof, hide — hide, quickly.

BEULAH   Where?

MOULSWORTH   Why?

SPY   Don't ask questions, and you will see. Hide, anywhere in the shadows.

(*He hides, too. The stage is peopled, but seems empty. Pause. The orchestra begins a waltz.* FREDDIE *and* MARFA *enter, obviously deeply in love. Gasps and whispers. A pause while they kiss.*)

FREDDIE   Are there words which have not been used before?

MARFA   There are silences which have not been shared before . . .

(*They embrace.*)

IGOR   (*hotly*) They're using our words.

JULIET   (*pained*) They've stolen our dialogue!

GENERAL   (*gently*) It is our country which is talking through their hearts, as before it talked through yours.

JULIET   You mean we invented nothing of our own?

GENERAL	You invented everything — even the country which is yours.
MARFA	Why do you look at me so critically?
FREDDIE	Me? I never criticize anything, on account of I have no opinions.
JULIET	(*affectionate*) Trust Freddie to break the spell.
MARFA	(*coquettish*) No opinions at all . . . then how do you know that you love me?
ROMANOFF	A logical question.
FREDDIE	I don't know, but I do.
MOULSWORTH	That's a pretty good blocking reply.
FREDDIE	Why do you love me?
BEULAH	Freddie's going right in there like a bulldozer.
MARFA	(*a little sigh*) I don't know, either. I haven't any reason. I have every reason not to love you. You are a capitalist. (*Amorously.*) What do you manufacture?
FREDDIE	Refrigerators, washing machines, vacuum cleaners.
MARFA	What volume of laundry can you wash at one time with your largest model?
FREDDIE	I don't know.
MARFA	And how much dirt is needed to fill the bag of your lightest vacuum cleaner?
FREDDIE	I don't know.
JULIET	(*irritated*) Oh, Freddie, try.
MARFA	You don't know . . . perhaps . . . perhaps I love you because you don't know . . . it's such a relief . . .
EVDOKIA	(*delighted*) Ah, the disease is taking root.

FREDDIE	You're a ship's captain, aren't you?
MARFA	(*with a sigh*) Yes . . .
FREDDIE	Gee, that's great . . .
MARFA	I'm captain of a sloop.
FREDDIE	Sloop. Sloop. That's a nice word. What's the tonnage?
MARFA	Why do you ask? You're not interested.
FREDDIE	No, that's right. I'm not. (*With a little laugh.*) I know what I like about you.
MARFA	What is it — (*Recklessly.*) — my love?
FREDDIE	Let me finish what I got to say, and then I'll kiss you. Of all the girls I've ever known you're the only one who could possibly be captain of a ship.
MARFA	The only one?
FREDDIE	My mother, she could have been an admiral — but you, you're the only one who could have been captain of a ship.
MARFA	(*her eyes shut*) I'm waiting.
FREDDIE	One other thing. How about you and me getting married?
MARFA	You're practical. I like that.
FREDDIE	I'm a capitalist.
MARFA	I hardly know you.
FREDDIE	That's why I ask you so soon.
MARFA	What would you do if I accept?
FREDDIE	I'd be very surprised.
MARFA	I accept.
FREDDIE	I'm very surprised.
	(*They kiss with increasing passion.*)

SPY   Proof enough?

                (*In silence*, HOOPER *kisses* BEULAH, VADIM
                kisses EVDOKIA.)

JULIET   I'm jealous of them already. I want it all to
                begin again.

IGOR   With all our agony?

JULIET   Oh, that was nothing . . .

                (*They kiss, too.*)

GENERAL   (*to the audience*) It is the night. Our
                victory is won. Do visit our country, if you
                can. The fare is as cheap as walking to the
                corner of the street to post a letter;
                accommodation is magnificent. All you
                need do is to shut your eyes, and in the
                night, with tranquil minds and softly
                beating hearts, you will find us here . . .
                the realm of sense, of gentleness, of love . . .
                the dream which every tortured modern
                man may carry in his sleep . . . our
                landscape is your pillow, our heavy
                industry — your snores . . .

                (*He retires in the darkness, and blows out
                the candles on the Altar. The music is a
                lullaby. The four love scenes continue in
                silence.*)

1ST SOLDIER   D.

2ND SOLDIER   R.

1ST SOLDIER   D. R. E.

2ND SOLDIER   A.

1ST SOLDIER   D. R. E. A . . . Oh . . .

2ND SOLDIER   Ah . . .

1ST SOLDIER   M.

2ND SOLDIER   One — love.

                Curtain.

PROPERTY PLOT

ACT ONE

On Stage: Piece of paper — 2ND SOLDIER
Watch — 2ND SOLDIER
Rifles — SOLDIERS
Carnival mask — GENERAL
Watch — 1ST SOLDIER
Various merchandise — SOLDIERS
Couple of rockets — 2ND SOLDIER
Few pieces of paper — SPY
American Magazine in pocket — IGOR

Off Stage: Black carnival mask — MOULSWORTH
Masks for IGOR and JULIET
Glass of water — MOULSWORTH

ACT TWO

On Stage: Various merchandise — SOLDIERS
Photo of Freddie in JULIET'S room
Empty photo frame
Pen and paper — JULIET
Sheets — IGOR
Bottle of whisky and glass — MOULSWORTH
Bottle of vodka and glass — ROMANOFF

Off Stage: Cigarettes and matches — FREDDIE
Handkerchief — BEULAH
Revolver — Igor
Watches — MOULSWORTH and ROMANOFF
Top hat, gloves, walking stick and portfolio
        — GENERAL
Typewritten document — MARFA

ACT THREE

On Stage: Hat from hat box — EVDOKIA
Rifles — SOLDIERS

Off Stage: Two life-size papier-mache figures — SOLDIERS

I

Words by
PETER USTINOV

Music by
ANTONY HOPKINS

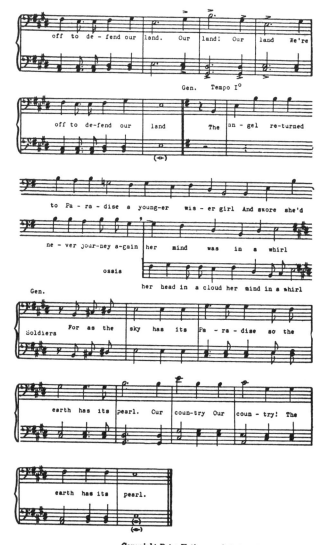

II

Words by
PETER USTINOV

Music by
ANTONY HOPKINS

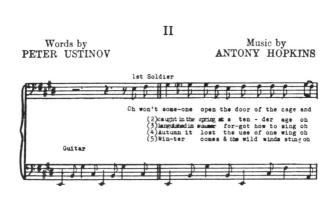

III

Words by
PETER USTINOV

Music by
ANTONY HOPKINS